NOTES of SERMONS

•

By

J. M. PENDLETON, D.D.

•

"But God forbid that I should glory save in the cross of our Lord Jesus Christ."—Galatians 6:14

•

Philadelphia
THE JUDSON PRESS
Chicago Los Angeles

Published by
THE JUDSON PRESS
Philadelphia 3, Pa.
20th thousand, January, 1955

Printed in U.S.A.

PREFACE

It is not often that the demand for a book of sermon outlines and notes continues for more than sixty years. Yet this has been true in the case of this volume by James Madison Pendleton, D.D., who for more than half a century served as a minister of the gospel in Baptist churches in Kentucky, Tennessee, Ohio, and Pennsylvania.

In the original preface to this book, Dr. Pendleton expressed his hope for it in the following words: "It has been prepared for the press with a desire that it may be useful to preachers who have not enjoyed the advantages of regular theological education. The author can readily imagine how such 'Notes' would have aided him in his early ministry, by way of suggestion as to the analysis of subjects and the construction of sermons. If he has done even a little to smooth for others the path which he often found rough, he does not regret his labor."

The reader will quickly discover that the sermon notes here presented have the ring of evangelical truth and evangelistic fervor. They bear something of the timeless character of the gospel itself in their universal appeal to ministers and Bible students of all generations. It is a privilege to republish them for the benefit of those ministers, young or old, who will welcome these suggestions for timely, biblical preaching.

MILES W. SMITH
Book Editor

SEPTEMBER 1, 1949

CONTENTS.

A

NOTES OF SERMONS.

NO BEING LIKE GOD.

Who is like unto thee, O Lord, among the gods? who is like thee, glorious in holiness, fearful in praises, doing wonders?—Exodus 15 : 11.

This is a part of what is called, in Rev. xv. 3, the song of Moses. It is a song of thanksgiving, of joy, and of triumph. There was enough to call it forth. The Israelites, pursued by Pharaoh and his hosts, and trembling in fear of destruction, saw the Red Sea open its waters and make a way for their escape. Their enemies followed with eager haste, and were utterly destroyed. "Then sang Moses and the children of Israel this song unto the Lord." They recognized his greatness, his power, and his glory. They saw his unapproachable superiority to all other beings, and said in the language of the text, "Who is like unto thee?" Theme—

NO BEING LIKE GOD.

Let us contemplate this truth. We are reminded of Paul's words in 1 Cor. viii. 5, 6, and of David's, in Psalm cxv. 3–8. These idol-gods were exalted by the ancient nations, but the true God is infinitely unlike them. Psalm lxxxix. 6. There can be but one God, and he is of necessity supreme in power and glory. The existence of one God renders impossible the existence of another. One being only can have existed from eternity; and from him all other beings must have derived their existence. Who, then, is like God? It is plain that in the exercise of creative omnipotence there is no likeness between him and any other being. But it will be more satisfactory to refer to the points brought out in the text in proof that there is no being like God.

I. *Glorious in holiness.* There is reference here to the moral perfections of God. The term holiness in its application to God is used in a limited, and in an enlarged sense. In its limited sense it denotes the purity of the divine nature, its absolute freedom from all taint of moral imperfection. In its enlarged sense it comprehends all the moral perfections of God, such as goodness, justice, veracity, etc. I think the Scriptures, to say the least, usually employ the term in the latter sense. The text favors this view. Why did Moses and the Israelites use the words, "glorious in holiness"? They saw the goodness of God in their deliverance, they saw his justice in the overthrow of their enemies, and they saw his truth in the fulfillment of his promises. In ascribing holiness to God, therefore, they not only attributed to him purity of nature, but all moral excellency. The holiness of God is expansible into all other moral perfections, and all other moral perfections are reducible to his holiness. This view will shed light on such passages as these: Psalm xlvii. 8; lxxxix. 35; Isaiah vi. 3; 1 Peter i. 16; Rev. iv. 8.

In saying that God is holy, the sacred writers virtually say that all moral perfection is his. You will observe that the text says he is *glorious* in holiness. That is, his holiness makes him glorious, or his holiness is his glory. If you say that each one of God's moral perfections is glorious, be it so; but when you consider his holiness as the union and the culmination of all these perfections, it is clearly seen to be the supreme glory of his character. If you regard the splendor radiating from this union and culmination as what the Bible calls "the beautv of holiness," you will perhaps have the correct view. In the fact that he is "glorious in holiness," there is no being like God.

II. *Fearful in praises.* These words teach an important truth, namely, that when God does that which calls forth our praise, we are to praise him with reverential awe. It is to be deplored that some persons address God in a familiar, flippant manner, almost as if they thought themselves his equals. God is to be feared while he is praised. The idea contained in the words "fearful in praises," is expanded in Psalm lxxxix. 7. God must have reverential praise. He is to be reverenced while he is praised.

III. *Doing wonders.* God did wonders in dividing the Red Sea. David tells that God alone does "wondrous things." In the highest sense this is true. The wondrous things done by all others are *comparatively* wonderful, and the power to do them comes from God. He performs wonders, and they are seen—

1. *In creation.* Seize the idea of creation, that is, the production of something out of nothing. The period was when there was nothing but God, I do not say in the universe, for there was no universe—nothing but God. There was no mind but his, and no matter at all. He willed to engage in the work of creation—to create matter and fashion it into worlds, to create angels, pure spirits, so far as we know, and men formed of matter and spirit. Think of the greatness and extent of creation—things visible and invisible. Say, does not God do wonders? Who is like him?

2. *In providence.* He upholds all things. To preserve what has been created requires the same power that created We must not forget God's providential wonders.

3. *In redemption.* What wonders are here! Eph. i 8; iii. 10; 1 Peter i. 12. There were problems connected with redemption which God only could solve. His wisdom gave the solution. His love prompted him to send his Son to die.

Myriads will be saved through Christ. What wonders will be seen in heaven!

REMARKS.

I. Love this infinitely glorious God.
II. Believe what he says.
III. Do what he commands.

GOD IS LIGHT.

. . . God is light, and in him is no darkness at all.—1 John i. 5.

Two of the sublimest expressions in the Bible are to be found in this Epistle. They are these: "God is love," and "God is light." The love and the light are in perfect concord. The love is co-extensive with the light, and the light is diffused through the love. There is a blessed interpenetration. The topic now to engage our attention is this:

GOD IS LIGHT.

While it is true that God is the Author of light in the literal sense of the word, the literal sense is not to be accepted in the text. The term light is here employed as a metaphor. It is clearly used in a figurative sense. Why? Because there is that in light which strikingly represents what is in God. Let us then consider light—

I. *As the symbol of knowledge.* By means of natural light we acquire knowledge. It makes us acquainted with a great variety of physical objects. How much we see by day,—the lovely flower and the majestic tree, the grassy mound and the towering mountain, the beautiful garden and the enrapturing prairie, the face of a friend and the blazing sun. By night we see the stars in their beauty and the moon in her glory. The telescope enlarges this circle of vision, but what could you see without light? I refer of course to natural light. Intellectual light acquaints us with matters in the realm of intellect. Spiritual light gives us knowledge of spiritual objects. Light in this threefold sense is the indispensable means of knowledge. It is therefore a fit symbol of knowledge. We see then why it is said that God is light. He has all knowledge. All the past is known to him, all the present, all the future. He knows all that angel or man has done, or said, or thought. He knows all that is taking place now in all worlds. He knows how you will feel at death, at the judgment, and through eternity. His knowledge is intuitive. 1 Chron. xxviii. 9; Acts xv. 18; Rom. xi. 33; 1 John iii. 20; Psalm cxxxix. 1–12. Surely if light is the symbol of knowledge, God is light. Darkness is the symbol of ignorance, and in him is no darkness at all.

II. *As the symbol of truth.* In Isaiah viii. 20, the word light seems to mean truth. There is such a connection between truth and knowledge that we cannot find out what is true unless we have knowledge. Light in its threefold sense enables us to know, so far as our finite faculties permit, what is true of things physical, intellectual, and spiritual. The limitations on our powers in the present state make it certain that more or less error will mix itself with the truth we learn; but in God there is no darkness at all. In the divine conceptions of truth there is no mistake, no error. Jehovah is the God of truth. Psalm xxxi. 5; c. 5. He is so the God of truth that when the Son came from the Father, he came "full of grace and truth"; and the Spirit proceeding from the Father and the Son is "the Spirit of truth." In the cross "mercy and truth have met together," and the gospel which proclaims this fact is emphatically the truth. The strong consolation of the saints arises from the fact that it "is impossible for God to lie." If then light is the symbol of truth, God is light.

III. *As the symbol of holiness.* Darkness symbolizes sin. Sinners are in darkness, and saints have been called out of darkness into marvelous light. Holiness, the opposite of sin, must be symbolized by light. God speaks from heaven concerning his holiness. 1 Peter i. 16. What said the seraphim? Isa. vi. 3. We are required to "worship the Lord in the beauty of holiness." Sin is the abominable thing which he hates. He cannot connive at it, and did not, even when Jesus died. He is so holy that he cannot permit our souls to enter heaven till cleansed from the last stain of sin; nor our bodies to appear there till raised from the grave in the image of the glorified body of Jesus. God is infinitely holy, and if light is the symbol of holiness, "God is light, and in him there is no darkness at all."

IV. *As the symbol of happiness and joy.* Darkness is the symbol of wretchedness and sorrow. The finally lost will be cast into "outer darkness." That light represents happiness and joy, we learn from Esther viii. 16; Psalm xcvii. 11; Isa. lviii. 8. God is called "the blessed God" (1 Tim. i. 11), and blessed here means happy. The joy of the Lord is the strength of his people. This joy is not only the joy of which he is the Author, but the joy which he feels. God's happiness is inconceivably great. Perhaps the best idea we can get of it is by pondering the words, "It is more blessed to give than to receive." This means that there is more happiness in giving than in receiving. To the truly benevolent, this is so. Now God gives, and his people receive. How much they receive on earth! But think of the happiness of saints and angels in heaven. God gives all this; and as it is more happy to give than to receive, God enjoys more happiness than all the souls on earth, and all the hosts of heaven. If light is the symbol of happiness and joy, God is light.

REMARKS.

I. Let us often think of God as light, and as "the Father of lights."

II. Let us aspire to fellowship with him, that we may not walk in darkness.

GOD A GENERAL AND A SPECIAL SAVIOUR.

. . . . The living God, who is the Saviour of all men, specially of those that believe.—1 Tim. iv. 10.

God has been pleased to refer in his word to himself under various designations, and these designations convey very important and precious ideas. It would be a profitable exercise to gather together all the terms and forms of expression used in the Bible as descriptive of the nature and the works of God. I do not think, however, that we should find a word more charmingly lovely and beautiful than Saviour. This is the prominent term in the text which presents to our view—

GOD A GENERAL AND A SPECIAL SAVIOUR.

To develop these two ideas is the work of this hour.

I. *God a general Saviour.* This is what is meant by the words, "Saviour of all men." But are these words to be understood absolutely? That is, will all men be saved? Surely not; for this view would render absurd the latter clause of the text. God is the Saviour of all men in these two senses:

1. *In providing salvation for all men.* The Scriptures teach that the provision made for the salvation of sinners is universal. The mission of Christ into the world had a gracious reference to the human race. John iii. 16; 1 John ii. 2. In the latter passage, John included himself among Jews, but also said, "the whole world," meaning Gentile nations. I know not how language could more strongly convey the idea of universality. God, in the gift of his Son, provides salvation for all men. The atonement of Christ has reference to all men. It has a reference to those who are

finally lost, which it has not to fallen angels. This fact is the only thing which justifies the universal proclamation of the gospel. This leads me to say that God is a general Saviour.

2. *In offering salvation to all men.* The offer follows the provision. The provision would be of no use without the offer, and the offer would be mockery without the provision. The following passages teach the offer of salvation tc all men: Mark xvi. 15; Luke xxiv. 46, 47; Titus ii. 11. Take these passages in their inverse order: The grace of God that brings salvation has appeared to all men. Repentance and remission of sins are to be preached among all nations. The gospel is to be preached in all the world, to every creature. Can language make it plainer that the offer of salvation is made to all men? In this sense God is the Saviour of all men. Even those who are finally lost are lost because of their rejection of salvation—a fact which of course proves that it was offered to them. You now see in what respects God is a general Saviour, the Saviour of all men.

II. *God a special Saviour.* "The Saviour of all men, specially of those that believe." Salvation provided and offered is not actual salvation. The former has to do with unbelievers, the latter with believers. The rich provisions of the gospel do not save unless they are accepted. There is nothing strange in this. The most ample feast does not satisfy the hunger of those who do not eat of it. Everywhere in connection with the gospel we read of faith, of believing. I may refer again to Mark xvi. 15, 16. The gospel is to be preached, but he that believeth and is baptized is to be saved. I call attention also to John iii. 14, 15. The lifting up of the Son of man on the cross includes the provision of salvation, but believing in him must follow to secure salvation. In other words, faith makes the possibilities of the cross actualities. There are several things implied in faith. There must be an object to believe in, and there must be a person to believe. Christ is prominently set forth as the object of faith, though there are a few passages which refer to faith as terminating on God. The text seems to be one of these: 1 Peter i. 21, certainly is. Faith reaches from him sent to him sending. The connection of salvation with faith shows the believer in Jesus to be a sinner. He needs salvation on this account; but he does not feel his need unless he feels that he is a sinner. For this reason I think repentance must precede faith. There is in repentance such a sense of the evil of sin and the ruin induced by it, as leads the sinner to feel his perishing need of salvation. Then the jailer's question is his, and the only answer is that of Paul. Acts xvi. 30, 31. Here then is an awakened sinner, and there is a gracious Saviour; but before there can be actual salvation the sinner and the Saviour must be brought together. How is this done? By faith. "Believe on the Lord Jesus Christ, and thou shalt be saved." Faith is the bond of union between Christ and the believer. Rom. x. 4. The gospel proclaims salvation, but it is "the power of God to salvation to every one that believeth." Rom. i. 16. Observe the limitation—a limitation of faith. Nothing that Jesus did during his life, nothing that he suffered on the cross, will avail to the salvation of an unbeliever. Infinite importance is attached to faith. Why? Chiefly because it is the means by which we receive Christ. He is offered as a Saviour, and the believer accepts the offer, thus responding to the gracious proposal God makes in the gospel. We see now how God is a special Saviour.

REMARKS.

I. I need not ask if God is your Saviour in the general sense.

II. But is he your Saviour in the special sense?

THE PROVIDENCE OF GOD.

For the eyes of the Lord run to and fro throughout the whole earth, to shew himself strong in the behalf of them whose heart is perfect toward him.—2 Chron. xvi. 9.

The kings of Israel and Judah were hostile to each other. This led Baasha, King of Israel, to build Ramah. His purpose is stated in verse 1. Asa, King of Judah, instead of looking to the Lord for help to defeat the scheme of Baasha, sent to Benhadad, King of Syria, for aid. He even took silver and gold out of the treasures of the house of the Lord to induce Benhadad to break his league with Baasha and send an army against the cities of Israel. Ver. 2, 3, 4. God was displeased with Asa because he relied on the King of Syria. Ver. 7. Asa was reminded of his former successes, which resulted from trusting in God. Then come the words of the text, suggestive of this topic:

THE PROVIDENCE OF GOD.

Let us notice—

I. *The doctrine of providence.* This is clearly taught in the Scriptures. It implies—

1. *The preservation of what God has made.* This accords with reason. God keeps in being what he was pleased to create. Creation and preservation are inseparable. Neh. ix. 6. God is Preserver. Psalm xxxvi. 6. In preserving his creatures, rational and irrational, he provides for their wants. Psalm civ. 27, 28; cxlvii. 9. God's vital power so pervades the universe that we live, move, and have our being in him. Should he withdraw his sustaining hand, all creatures would sink into nothingness.

2. *The control of what he has made.* This differs from preservation, though it includes it. God exercises dominion over all his works. His work of creation gives him the right of control, and this right he does not transfer. All things and

all beings are in his hands. His providence is universal. He controls the movements of every planet and the fall of every sparrow. He gives light to the sun in the heavens and to the glow-worm on the earth. He is God over all.

3. *The ordering of all events.* Of these events, so far as we are concerned, we may begin with—

a. The time and place of our birth. If we ask why we were not born a thousand years ago? why our birth-place was not different? why we did not descend from different parents?—we can only say: The Lord did not so order it. Can you give any other answer?

b. Occurrences during life. These are more or less numerous in the life of every person. Of all things it may be said that God does them, or permits them to be done. Some are rich and some poor. Some who were rich have become poor, and *vice versa.* You have had health and sickness, prosperity and adversity. You know not what is yet before you, but God will order it.

c. The time and place of death. Of the time, we can say, that it will soon come; of the place, we can say nothing certain. Were it possible, we might feel curious to know *when* and *where* we shall die, whether in one year or in twenty, whether at home or abroad, on the land or on the sea. God will order this.

II. *God's providence specially favors those whose hearts are right.* What says the text? The language seems to imply that the eyes of the Lord are intent on looking throughout the whole earth, to see if there are any of his servants who stand in special need of his help. A perfect heart, in the sense of the text, is a heart whose reliance on God is unreserved. See ver. 8. When Asa relied thus on the Lord, chariots and horsemen and armies were put to flight. "He delivered them into thy hand." When the hearts of God's people are right he shows himself strong in their behalf. In his arm is everlasting strength. He shows himself strong in behalf of his people:

1. *By defeating the designs of their enemies.* This was seen in national Israel. Ex. xv. 9–12. God showed himself strong. He does the same thing in behalf of his spiritual Israel. With infinite ease he can thwart the purposes of his enemies and the enemies of his people.

2. *By overruling the acts of their enemies for good.* Paul refers to a case of this kind in Phil. i. 12. The cause of Christ was promoted by the persecution which Paul suffered.

3. *By nerving them to the performance of duty.* Acts xxvi. 22.

4. *By sustaining them under temptation.* 1 Cor. x. 13.

5. *By delivering them out of trouble.* Psalm l. 15.

6. *By blessing them in death.* Rev. xiv. 13.

7. *By imparadising them in heaven.* 2 Cor. v. 8; Phil. i. 23.

Jehovah–Jesus says, "Fear not, little flock; for it is your Father's good pleasure to give you the kingdom." Luke xii. 32. "Father, I will that those also whom thou hast given me, be with me where I am; that they may behold my glory." John xvii. 24. The Lord is strong to deliver his people from all evil and preserve them unto his heavenly kingdom.

REMARKS.

I. The doctrine of Providence is full of consolation. We are under the dominion of neither fate nor chance. An all-wise and gracious God has the scepter of the universe in his hands. Who would have that scepter elsewhere?

II. The providence of God is universal. "The eyes of the Lord run to and fro throughout the whole earth." They are in every place. We have to live in different places, in places remote, it may be, from one another. Our eyes can be in but one place. The eyes of the Lord are in every place, and there is his omnipotent arm to protect.

THE WONDERFUL CHRIST.

And his name shall be called Wonderful.—Isa. ix. 6.

Whose name? The name of him referred to in this verse as the "child born,' "the Son given," the mighty God," "the Prince of peace." There is but one Being in the universe to whom these words can be applied, namely, Christ. We direct our contemplations then to—

THE WONDERFUL CHRIST.

In showing that he is wonderful, I shall refer to some aspects of his person, character, and work of mediation. I may say that he is wonderful—

I. *In his person.* We must not forget that he is the God-man. His person is therefore unique. It is obvious that he is the God-*man*, because he was originally God. Had he been originally man he never could have become the God-man. That is to say, humanity could never have taken divinity into union with itself; but divinity did form an alliance with humanity. The union of the two natures constituted the person of the Christ, or, the Christ himself. It will be seen therefore that in his person the widest extremes of being meet, the finite and the infinite. Surely he is wonderful in his person.

II. *In his character.* A man's character is what he is. He was pleased while on earth to call himself "the Son of man." This designation denotes his relation to the human race, but he escaped the corruption of the race by a miraculous assumption of our nature. All human virtues in their sinless integrity belong to him, and all divine excellences are his. His character therefore exhibits all the majestic glories of supreme divinity and all the milder glories of incorrupt humanity. Without doubt such a character is wonderful.

III. *In his love.* It is wonderful that he loved fallen men at all, and that he loved them in preference to fallen angels. Whence the origin of this love? What caused it? We know not. Whence its discrimination between angels and men? We know not. We only know that he who is wonderful so loved sinners of Adam's race that he was willing to leave his throne in heaven and come to earth on the errand of salvation. He knew the sacrifices inseparable from his incarnation. Indeed, his incarnation itself was a sacrifice of colossal proportions. The wonderful Christ was prompted by wonderful love in all he did.

IV. *In his death.* He became incarnate in order that he might die. The manner in which his death was brought about was wonderful. It was instigated by Satan, facilitated by Judas, insisted on by the Jews, and accomplished by Pilate. They all acted freely, but he died according to the purpose of God, and he died voluntarily. He laid down his life for his enemies, and his death was an atoning death, designed to sustain the majesty of the divine law and satisfy the claims of offended justice. That Christ is wonderful is seen in his death.

V. *In the power of his influence.* The name cast out as evil, despised and execrated when he died, has more influence than all other names; and this influence is destined to increase till the world is filled with it. Men, Christians, and infidels are constantly writing "Lives of Christ," but they cannot exhaust the theme. Our literature and our laws are pervaded by the influence of Christ's name. It is a name above every name, and the power of his influence proclaims him the wonderful Christ.

VI. *In the salvation of countless multitudes.* Without enlarging on this point, I merely refer to Rev. v. 9; vii. 9, 10

REMARKS.

I. What think you of this wonderful Christ?

II. What you think of him determines whether you are a saint or a sinner.

III. It is a great thing to have Christ as a personal Saviour.

IV. It is better not to be born than to live and die "without Christ."

ABRAHAM REJOICING TO SEE THE DAY OF CHRIST.

Your father Abraham rejoiced to see my day; and he saw it, and was glad.—John viii. 56.

There was nothing in which the Jews rejoiced more than in their lineal descent from Abraham. They were proud of their relationship to him. Even when their unbelief and disobedience reached the highest point, they boasted of their connection with the man who was remarkable for his faith and obedience. This was a strange inconsistency. The Jews rejected Christ when he came, but Abraham looked forward to his coming with the deepest interest and the devoutest joy. This we learn from the text. My subject will be—

ABRAHAM REJOICING TO SEE THE DAY OF CHRIST.

It will be proper to inquire:

I. *How Abraham saw the day of Christ.* There can be no reference to literal vision. Abraham lived many centuries before the coming of Christ. He did not and could not see the day of Christ as the disciples of Jesus saw it. But there was a sense in which he saw it, namely:

1. *By the anticipation of faith.* He, like other Old Testament saints, "died in faith," and, of course, lived in faith. His faith was founded on the promises of God. It could have no other basis on which to rest. With this basis he looked through the long vista of intervening years and saw the accomplishment of what God had said. The promise to

Abraham is recorded first in Gen. xii. 3: "In thee shall all the families of the earth be blessed." There is a renewal of the promise in Gen. xviii. 18; xxii. 18, and in these passages there is a substitution of "nations" for "families." "In thee" does not mean in Abraham, personally, but in his seed. When we turn to the New Testament we find this great promise quoted again and again; and we learn from Gal. iii. 16, what "seed" means. We see the important difference between the singular and the plural number. "He saith not, And to seeds, as of many; but as of one, And to thy seed, which is Christ." This brings the matter to a point. Christ was the seed. Abraham saw in anticipation that he was to have an illustrious descendant, who would be the central figure of history, and the hope of the world. It may be said that he saw the day of Christ whenever—

a. He made a sacrificial offering to God. The rite of sacrifice was instituted immediately after the fall. This rite was observed by Abel, Noah, and Abraham, and was made prominent in the Mosaic Economy. Abraham knew that every sacrifice was a type, and that the antitype would be found in his "seed," the Messiah. He hailed his coming as the "substance" of which the type was the "shadow." With him the shedding of the blood of animals was prophetic of the shedding of the blood of the atoning Lamb who was to be manifested in "the fulness of time."

b. When he offered his son Isaac on the altar. Of this we have an account in Genesis xxii. The command of God was positive, unprecedented, and hard for a father to obey. Plausible objections might have been urged, but Abraham did not urge them. He built an altar, laid wood in order, bound Isaac, and placed him "on the altar upon the wood." He took the knife and stretched forth his hand to slay his son. Never did man more fully intend to do a thing. The angel of the Lord arrested the hand of the father, and rescued the son. The attention of Abraham was directed to a ram caught in a thicket by the horns; and this animal was offered in the place of Isaac. Here we have substitution, and the patriarch, in seeing the day of Christ, saw that in him would be exemplified the doctrine of substitution as never before and never after. If, as is probable, the angel was the angel of the covenant, the pre-incarnate Saviour, we may imagine what he said to Abraham. We may suppose, too, that light so clear was shed on the mystery of the distant incarnation as to enable Abraham to see, more fully than before, the day of Christ. Faith became so strong in its anticipatory power as to be equivalent to sight. Thus did the father of the faithful see the day of Christ.

II. *Abraham rejoiced to see Christ's day.* Notice the words "rejoiced" and "was glad." The very day that afforded the unbelieving Jews no pleasure Abraham rejoiced to see, though only in anticipation. Why did he rejoice? There was abundant reason for his joy—

1. *He saw that the day of Christ was to have a vital connection with his own salvation.* He knew that the seed of the woman (Gen. iii. 15) was to be his seed, and this seed was to be the great depositary of his personal salvation. No hope for him apart from Christ, who was to descend from his loins. We can see that Abraham had the best personal reason for his joy.

2. *He saw that the day of Christ was to have an important connection with the best interests of his lineal descendants.* He had been told that he was to have a numerous posterity. Though many temporal blessings were to be enjoyed by his descendants, their salvation from sin and its consequences was the great matter to be made possible through the ushering in of the day of Christ. This day, it is true, was to be darkened by the deep shadows of his death, but destined to shine brighter after his resurrection.

3. *He saw that the day of Christ would have a world-wide influence for good.* "In thee shall all the families of the earth be blessed"; that is as we have seen, in Christ. The proclamation of mercy was to be made to the whole human race, from the rising of the sun to the far west, from the equator to the poles. This was to be done through Abraham's seed and Abraham's Lord. Well did the patriarch rejoice to see the day of Christ.

REMARKS.

I. The day to which Abraham looked has come.

II. Another day, the day of judgment, will come.

III. A right improvement of the former prepares for the latter.

THE DEATH OF CHRIST.

Who appeared in glory, and spake of his decease which he should accomplish at Jerusalem.—Luke ix. 31.

Without hesitation I may say that the death of Christ is the most important event that has ever taken place on earth. His cross is invested with a grandeur all its own. It attracts the attention of all the redeemed, and angels study its mysteries of grace. Doubtless, the death of Jesus is the theme of many of the colloquies of heaven. On this theme dwelt Moses and Elijah on the Mount of Transfiguration. They were clothed with glory. They shone with a splendor like that of heaven. Rays of divinity darted through the vail of the Redeemer's humanity. His countenance was changed and his raiment became white as snow. What a scene! Moses and Elijah were very properly present; the former the representative of the law; the latter, of the prophets. They appeared to do honor to the Magnifier of the law and the Fulfiller of the predictions of the prophets. These two men had been for centuries in heaven, had seen much, had heard much, had learned much, but knew of nothing so full of interest as the "decease" of Christ about to take place at Jerusalem. This was the topic on which they dwelt, and I dwell on it to-day.

THE DEATH OF CHRIST.

I inquire into—

I. *The cause of his death.* This we find in the love of God. We have the testimony of Jesus himself on this point as follows: "For God so loved the world, that he gave his only begotten Son, that whosoever believeth in him should not perish, but have everlasting life." John iii. 16. There is a blessed repetition of this teaching in Rom. v. 8; 1 John iv. 10. Of the strength of this love we can form only a feeble conception. If all the love of all the angels could be concentrated into one heart, there would be unspeakably less love in that heart than God felt for ruined man when he sent his own Son on a mission of mercy. Remember, that the Son of God had been from eternity the object of his Father's complacent affection and delight. Isa. xlii. 1. But love to this world induced the Father to give up his Son. We must not suppose that God's love to sinners was excited by the death of Christ. This would be transposing cause and effect. The death of Christ would not have occurred at all had there not been previous love in the bosom of God. The gift of Christ is God's "unspeakable gift," but his love was antecedent to the gift, and the gift is emphatically traceable to the love.

II. *The nature of Christ's death.* On this point opinions differ. Unitarians and Socinians concede that Christ's death manifests the love of God and confirms the truth of what Jesus taught, but they exclude from it all idea of atonement. They deny that his sufferings were expiatory, and say that expiation was needless. They make the greatest of all mistakes; for it is a soul-destroying mistake. The grand peculiarity of the death of Christ is its expiatory nature

He died as a propitiation, died to atone for sin. This is manifest from such Scriptures as these: "Whom God has set forth as a propitiation through faith in his blood." "Once in the end of the world hath he appeared to put away sin by the sacrifice of himself." "Who his own self bare our sins in his own body on the tree." "And he is the propitiation for our sins, and not for ours only, but also for the sins of the whole world." Rom. iii. 25; Heb. ix. 26; 1 Peter ii. 24; 1 John ii. 2. The death of Christ was an atoning death. Had it not been, there would have been no saving value in it.

III. *The necessity of Christ's death.* I do not refer to absolute necessity, for there was not such necessity. God might justly have permitted fallen men to perish in their sins, as he did fallen angels. He was under no obligation to save them. By the necessity of the death of Christ, I mean that it was necessary to render the salvation of sinners consistent with the law and justice of God. I have said that the love of God was the cause of the death of Christ. Of course the atonement of Jesus does not make God merciful, but it enables him to exercise his mercy without compromising the rectitude and the honor of his government. Some vainly talk about the efficacy of repentance to atone for sin. There is no such efficacy. Has repentance ever been regarded in civil governments as expiatory of crime? Can repentance repair physical or moral injury? But it is folly to talk of the efficacy of repentance, in view of the fact that no sinner ever repents independently of influences proceeding from the atonement of Christ. No created being could atone for sin. The universal law of creatureship is that all which creatures can render is due to God on their own account. This makes creature substitution impossible. Atonement, therefore, if made at all, must be made by a being above the law of creatureship, having the sovereign right of self-disposal. In other words, he who makes atonement for sin must be divine.

IV. *The results of the death of Christ.* I can merely refer to some of these. I name the following:

1. *The offer of salvation is made to all men.* Jesus himself says: "Thus it is written, and thus it behooved Christ to suffer, and to rise from the dead the third day: And that repentance and remission of sins should be preached in his name among all nations." Luke xxiv. 46, 47. The death of Christ, the sacrificial value of which was proved by his resurrection, is the basis of the proclamation of the gospel. Salvation is offered to men with indiscriminate universality. There is no difference between the Jew and the Greek. There is nothing in the way of the salvation of any man but his unwillingness to be saved by Christ.

2. *The Holy Spirit is given.* He is sent to reprove the world of sin. It is his province to give life to the sinner, dead in sin. He renews the heart, sanctifies the soul, and fits it for heaven.

3. *The actual salvation of countless myriads.* We cannot tell what proportion of the human race will be saved. We know, however, that redemption in every case will result from the death of Christ. Rev. v. 9. His *death* will be *life* to all the saved.

4. *The divine glory will be pre-eminently promoted.* The glory of God is the supreme end of all he does. Creation and providence display his glory, but redemption through the death of Christ far, far more.

REMARKS.

I. Think and talk much of this great topic.

II. It will be the grandest theme of heaven.

CHRIST FORSAKEN OF GOD.

My God, my God, why hast thou forsaken me?—Matt. xxvii. 46.

If this is the language of complaint, it stands alone in its relation to the sufferings of Christ. When his enemies seized and bound him, there was on his part no complaint. When they put a crown of thorns on his head, mocked him, spit upon him, smote him, he said not a word. When scourged by order of Pilate, he was silent. When nailed to the cross, there was no word of remonstrance. His bodily sufferings seemed to have made scarcely any impression on him. It has been well said that "the sufferings of his soul were the soul of his sufferings." These sufferings, so fearful in Gethsemane, became more intense on the cross, and reached their terrible climax when the words of the text were uttered.

CHRIST FORSAKEN OF GOD.

This solemn topic is the theme of our meditations. Let us inquire—

I. *How was Christ forsaken?* There was, of course, no withdrawal of the essential presence of God. This was simply impossible. God is everywhere. Psalm cxxxix. 7–11. His glorious presence in heaven, his gracious presence on earth, and his avenging presence in hell, are all dependent on his essential presence. When, therefore, Christ was forsaken of God, we must understand that he was left without that ineffable communion which he, as the second person of the Godhead, had enjoyed with the first from eternity. Of this divine communion the most exalted creatures can form only a feeble conception. There is what Rev. John Harris calls "society in the Godhead." The social bliss enjoyed by the Sacred Three no finite thought can reach. Our attention is directed in the text, not to the Spirit, but the Father and the Son. Manifestly the Son had ever basked in the smiles of the Father's face. There had been undisturbed union in nature, in love, in purpose, between the two. Out of this union grew communion infinite and glorious, knowing no suspension till the tragedy of Calvary occurred. Then God forsook the Son of his love. The manifestations of his loving presence were suspended. Communion with heaven was interrupted. What an hour was that! Christ suffering death at the hands of his enemies, deserted by his friends, angels impotent to help, and forsaken by his God! He was not forsaken in the sense that the supports of divinity were withdrawn from him, but in the sense that God hid his face from him, and left him in the excruciating loneliness which was never known before and never will be known again. Well may we ask—

II. *Why Christ was thus forsaken?*

It was necessary in order—

1. *That his death might be an atoning death.* By such a death I mean that satisfaction be rendered to the law and justice of God, so that pardoning mercy can consistently reach the guilty. But this implies three things, namely, that Christ died for the guilty, that he was held answerable for them, and that his sufferings were inflicted by the Lawgiver, God. If he had not died for sinners, there could have been no atonement. If the Divine Government had not accepted him as the substitute for sinners, there could have been no atonement. If the Lawgiver had not inflicted the death, there would have been no atoning quality in it. All these essentials to atonement are found in the death of Christ. I refer now more specially to the last. God, the Lawgiver, inflicted on Christ his atoning sufferings and death. Isa. liii. 6, 10; Zech. xiii. 7; Rom. iii. 25. Death was the penalty of the law; not natural death merely, but in a much higher sense, spiritual death. Jesus would not have met the penalty of the law if he had not died in both senses

Now when God forsook him, he suffered spiritual death. He was separated from God and made a curse for men. This was to him death in an infinitely more awful sense than the death of his body. Hear his words: "My God, my God, why hast thou forsaken me?" Such a death, the death of such a Being, conferred greater honor on the law than would the eternal perdition of the millions of the saved.

2. *That God might show his estimate of sin.* It is the abominable thing which he hates. Of this he has given many proofs, beginning with the expulsion of rebellious angels. But when he forsook Christ on the cross he gave an emphasis to his estimate of sin which the revolutions of eternity will not disturb. Sin was charged to Christ by imputation, iniquity was laid upon him, he was a sin-offering. While Christ was in himself altogether lovely, sin imputed to him and resting on him was so hateful that God was obliged to turn from the sight, and in so doing forsook his only begotten Son. In this fact the universe can see God's estimate of sin.

3. *That sinners might not be forsaken forever.* Because God forsook his Son he can take sinners to his heart. It was because he loved the world that he gave his Son, and having given him laid on him our iniquities. What wonders are these, that because Christ was forsaken we are brought near to God, accepted as righteous for Jesus' sake, adopted into the family of God, treated as children, and made heirs of heavenly glory!

REMARKS.

I. Despair not, Christian, if sometimes you seem forsaken of God.

II. You will be with him forever in heaven.

III. Alas for those whom God will forsake eternally.

THE DEATH OF CHRIST THE MEANS OF REDEMPTION IN ALL AGES.

And for this cause he is the mediator of the new testament, that by means of death, for the redemption of the transgressions that were under the first testament, they which are called might receive the promise of eternal inheritance.—Heb. ix. 15.

I assume without discussion that testament in this text signifies covenant. The original word has this meaning, and is often translated covenant in the New Testament, and should perhaps be so rendered in every place. If any exception is to be made it must be in the two verses following the text. It is doubtful in regard to them. The text presents as our theme—

THE DEATH OF CHRIST THE MEANS OF REDEMPTION IN ALL AGES.

Please direct your attention first to this truth:

I. *Christ is Mediator of the new covenant.* The Hebrews were partial to the old covenant, because Moses was its mediator, and because its administration was provided for under the Mosaic Economy. The reverence of the Jews for their lawgiver was great. They gloried in the law ordained by angels in his hands. But there is a better covenant, established on better promises. That is to say, better things are promised, and there is better security for the performance of what is promised. Christ is Mediator. In some respects he is like Moses; in other respects, totally unlike him, as we shall see under the next division of the subiect. Moses administered the old covenant; Christ administers the new. Moses stood between God and the Jewish people; Christ stands between God and the human race. The old covenant had to do with one nation; the new has to do with all nations. In the highest sense of mediation there is one Mediator between God and men, the man Christ Jesus As he possesses the nature of both parties between whom he interposes, we may be sure of his fitness and competency to carry into effect all the purposes of his interposition.

II. *The Mediator's death the means of redemption in all ages.* Here we may see the unlikeness between Christ and Moses. The latter did not redeem his people by means of his death. Their redemption was specially dependent on his active life while engineering their deliverance from the bondage of Egypt. His death, so far as we can see, would have prevented their redemption. Christ's work of redemption was dependent on his death. I do not mean that there was not value in his teachings, in his blameless life, and perfect example. I attribute to these all the worth the Scriptures assign them. But I mean to say that the death of Christ was indispensable to the spiritual redemption of sinners, even as the death of the paschal lamb was to the literal redemption of Israel from Egypt. The sacrifices of the law were essential to the remission of ceremonial offences and ceremonial penalties. There was no *real* atonement, but only a *typical* one, by means of any sacrifice. Now Christ by his sacrificial death made a real atonement, and all the sacrifices of the law considered as types found in him their antitype. The death of animals offered in sacrifice was essential to the removal of ceremonial iniquity from Jewish transgressors. So the death of Christ is indispensable to the removal of moral offences. You will note that sins "under the first covenant" were expiated by means of the death of Christ. Hence the words "redemption of the transgressions that were under the first covenant." This means redemption of the transgressors, so that it follows that all sinners saved under the Mosaic Economy, and also from the days of Adam, were saved by means of the death of Christ. We know also that all saved since the Saviour died have been saved through his death. How conspicuous stands his cross! Old Testament saints looked forward to it; New Testament saints look back to it. The attention of all the redeemed of all ages has been attracted by its glory. We may learn much from Rom. iii. 25, 26.

III. *The called receive promise of eternal inheritance.* "They who are called," more correctly, "have been called." This is "the heavenly calling." The Israelites had an earthly calling, were called to an earthly inheritance. Christians are called to a heavenly inheritance. This calling is equivalent to regeneration, as we may see from 1 Cor. i. 24; Gal. i. 15; 2 Tim. i. 9. As the result of the calling we are brought into a filial relation to God. We become the children of God by faith in Christ Jesus. There is a hope connected with this calling, as we see in Eph. i. 18. The calling creates hope and directs attention to an inheritance. Notice the words, "receive the promise." The promise is made to the called, and they are, therefore, within its scope. See what is promised—an inheritance, an eternal, or rather, the eternal inheritance. There is only one eternal inheritance, and the called have promise of it. It is "the inheritance of the saints in light," "among the sanctified," "incorruptible, undefiled, and that fadeth not away." The called are to inherit a kingdom (Matt. xxv. 34), and to inherit eternal life (Titus iii. 7). Many of the poor are among the called, but how rich they are!

REMARKS.

I. How great are our obligations to Christ!

II. Let us not forget that his death is our life and our salvation.

III. Let us live consistently with our heirship of glory.

IV. Through the death of Christ is the only hope for any of Adam's race.

THE SON OF MAN LIFTED UP.

And as Moses lifted up the serpent in the wilderness, even so must the Son of man be lifted up; that whosoever believeth in him should not perish, but have eternal life.—John iii. 14, 15.

The following points are worthy of attention:

I. *What called for the lifting up of the serpent in the wilderness, and what for the lifting up of the Son of man.*

II. *The lifting up of the serpent and the lifting up of the Son illustrate the goodness of God.*

III. *The cure of the bitten Israelite was dependent on his looking to the brazen serpent; the salvation of sinners is suspended on faith in Christ.*

IV. *The result in each case—the wounded Israelite healed, the sinner saved from perishing and made heir of eternal life.*

V. *The Israelite who refused to look to the brazen serpent died, and deserved no sympathy; the sinner who rejects Christ perishes, and forfeits all claim to the sympathies of the universe.*

REMARKS.

I. The need of a Saviour is universal.

II. We should be devoutly thankful that a Saviour has been provided.

III. All should gladly accept him.

IV. Those who reject him incur fearful guilt and danger.

CHRIST'S ABILITY TO SAVE.

Wherefore he is able also to save them to the uttermost that come unto God by him, seeing he ever liveth to make intercession for them.—Heb. vii. 25.

This chapter contains an impressive contrast between the Levitical priesthood and the priesthood of Jesus Christ. The superiority of the latter is clearly shown. There is under the gospel economy a change of the priesthood. There is a change as to the tribe officiating—formerly Levi, now Judah. There is a change as to the manner of consecration to office, not by a carnal commandment, but by an oath. There is a change as to the moral qualifications for office. Levitical priests were men of infirmity; Christ is holy, harmless, undefiled. There is a change as to the duration of the priesthood. Levitical priests were removed by death, but Christ continueth ever. These facts are a suitable introduction to the subject brought to view in the text, namely:

CHRIST'S ABILITY TO SAVE.

His ability to save may be seen in view of the following points:

I. *His removal of all legal obstructions out of the way of the salvation of sinners.* By legal obstructions I of course mean the impediments, the hindrances interposed by the law of God. The law had been broken. To violate its precepts was to incur its penalty. In the jurisprudence of Heaven, "the wages of sin is death." The law asserted its claims and demanded either the execution of its penalty on personal transgressors, or the adoption of some measure that would be recognized in the Divine Government as an equivalent. Such a measure was found in the obedience and death of Christ. His sacrifice answers, and, by a blessed necessity, far more than answers, all the purposes that would have been answered if those who are saved had personally suffered the curse of the law. Indeed, the death of Jesus, by reason of the dignity of his person, honors the law infinitely more than would the punishment of sinners. The atonement of Christ obviates every legal difficulty in the way of the salvation of sinners. Hence I argue his ability to save.

II. *He has provided for the removal of the moral obstructions out of the way of the salvation of sinners.* These obstructions are to be found in the depravity of the heart, its opposition to

God and holiness. "The carnal mind is enmity against God." The heart is "desperately wicked." These moral obstructions, unless removed, will as certainly prevent the salvation of sinners as would the legal obstructions, had they not been removed. It is the province of the Holy Spirit to remove these moral obstacles. This is his work, and his agency is indispensable. What he does in renewing the heart is referred to as a creation and a resurrection—two things obviously possible to divine power only. But the gift and the work of the Holy Spirit have been secured through the mediation of Jesus. Now remember that these two classes of obstructions, legal and moral, are exhaustive of all impediments in the way of salvation, and we see in their removal Christ's ability to save.

III. *His ability to save is seen in the countless multitude of the subjects of his grace.* We know not what myriads before his incarnation had a prospective saving interest in his advent. We are sure that numberless millions since his coming have been redeemed by his blood. Old Testament saints were saved by a Saviour to come, and New Testament saints are saved by a Saviour who has come—one and the same Saviour. His cross stands in conspicuous majesty and glory. He has saved sinners of all classes, the young, the middle aged, the old, the wise, the ignorant, the tender-hearted, the hard-hearted, the amiable, and the repulsive. Among all these classes the saving efficacy of his blood has been seen. How many are the subjects of his grace now on earth, and how greatly will the number increase before the end of the world! During the millenial period those saved by him will be as the drops of morning dew. The text says "he is able to save to the uttermost," that is, completely, fully, in extreme cases. All this shows his ability to save.

.V. *He ever lives to make intercession.* This is the reason assigned in the text. His atonement is the basis of his intercession. He lives to carry into full accomplishment the objects contemplated in his death. He lives to preside over the interests confided to his charge. He is able to save, because he is a living Saviour, a living Intercessor. His priesthood passes not away, but abides unchangeable amid the mutations of time. As he lives, he can save those that die. Refer to Rom. v. 10.

CHRIST'S ABILITY TO SAVE IS EXERTED IN BEHALF OF THOSE ONLY WHO COME TO GOD BY HIM.

Coming to God by a priest, through a sacrifice under the Mosaic law, was typical of coming to God by Christ. This coming is a movement, not of the body, but of the soul. It implies the sinner's departure from, and his return to, God. The Father must be approached through the Son; for Jesus says, "no man cometh to the Father but by me." But why is Christ's mediatorial power to save exerted in behalf of those only who come to God by him? I give two reasons for this:

I. *If it was exerted in behalf of others, there would be a virtual encouragement of impenitence.* Coming to God implies repentance, whatever else it may imply. Those who come to God are tired of sin; they hate it, and are sorry for it. In their repentance originates their purpose to return to God, and they do return, even as the repenting prodigal (Luke xv.) returned to his father. In coming to God their hearts are broken with sorrow that they have sinned against him; and then Jesus exerts his power in saving them, and not *till then.* Now if coming to God implies repentance, it is plain that if Christ should exercise his saving power in behalf of those who do not come to God, there would be a virtual encouragement of impenitence. But to encourage sin in any of its forms would be in antagonism with the character of Christ and with all the purposes of his mediatorial work.

II. *If Christ saved those who do not come to God by him, he would deviate from the gospel plan and nullify his own mediation.* This is of course impossible. Christ cannot thwart the gospel plan of saving sinners. He cannot make his own mediation of no effect; for this would be a virtual denial of the necessity of his death; it would be a virtual declaration that the erection of his cross on Calvary was needless. The denial and the declaration are impossible, and therefore Christ exerts his power to save in behalf of those only who come to God by him.

REMARKS.

I. This subject is full of comfort to Christians.

II. It is replete with interest to those who are asking the great question, "What must I do to be saved?"

III. Let the impenitent tremble, knowing that Christ is able to *destroy* as well as to save, and that he will destroy all who do not come to God by him

---

THE DIMENSIONS OF CHRIST'S LOVE.

May be able to comprehend with all saints what is the breadth, and length, and depth, and height; and to know the love of Christ.—Eph. iii. 18, 19.

This is a part of Paul's prayer for the Ephesian Church. It is a wonderful prayer, vastly comprehensive. He prays that the members of this church might be "strengthened with might by the Spirit," that Christ might "dwell in their hearts by faith," and that they might be "rooted and grounded in love." The attainment of all the rich blessings included in these petitions prepares for something to follow, namely: Ability to comprehend what is the breadth, length, depth, and height of the love of Christ. The theme furnished by these words is a delightful one. It is—

THE DIMENSIONS OF CHRIST'S LOVE.

It will be our business, then, not only to fix our thoughts on the love of Christ, but to measure it. You say it is im measurable. So it is. You cannot fully measure it; but make the best measurement you can. Engage in the delightfully impossible work of measuring the measureless. To make your measurement methodical, follow the order of the text.

I. *Breadth.* This term is the opposite of narrowness. Certainly there is nothing contracted in Christ's love. One of the objects of Paul in this epistle was to show this. He tells us of the mystery hidden from ages, but revealed by the gospel, that Gentiles and Jews should be fellow-heirs and partakers of the same grace. The Jewish conception of the Messiah's love was, that it would encircle in its embrace all the tribes of Israel, and make no provision for the salvation of Gentiles. The apostles, too, had this view, with the commission of Christ before them. Matt. xxviii. 19; Mark xvi. 15. Their prejudices suggested a narrow interpretation. By "all the world," they probably understood all the Holy Land, and by "all nations," all the Jewish tribes. A miracle was necessary to overcome Peter's prejudices. Acts x. In opposition to the Jewish view, the love of Christ is world-wide. It takes hold of the Gentile as well as the Jew. No nation is outside of its operation. Neither culture nor ignorance is in its way, nor any form of government, nor any peculiar traits of character. It recognizes no lines of latitude or longitude. Its sceptre extends from the equator to the poles. Is there not breadth in this love? He who reaches heaven will see what John saw. Rev. vii. 9.

II. *Length.* This term indicates another measurement.

It leads us to inquire how long this love has been exercised, and how long it will be exercised. We can trace it back through all the ages. Let us take our stand on Calvary, and look backward and forward. Backward we go, through prophecy, sacrifices, types, and shadows, to the Garden of Eden; and in that garden we find the first intimation of mercy to man. Gen. iii. 15. But we must go farther back; for this love antedates creation. Jer. xxxi. 3; 2 Tim. i. 9; Titus i. 2. When we get to a period anterior to the creation of the world, that period is equivalent to the words, *from eternity.* The love of Christ did not exhaust its power on the cross. It did not die when the great Lover died. It presided over his sepulchre, and triumphed in his resurrection. It has bestowed the blessings of salvation thus far along the tracks of time. Jesus, having loved his own, loves them to the end, to the end of life, to the end of time, and then will love them in heaven forever. As to the love of Christ in its length I can only say, *from eternity to eternity.*

III. *Depth.* Another measurement still. We may consider the depth of Christ's love in connection with the deep ruin from which it delivers. The miseries of the fall are deep miseries. Sinners are deeply involved in guilt and condemnation. They are sunk deep in depravity and pollution. The holiness of God being the standard of perfection, how far are sinners below that standard! How deep their degradation by sin! The depth of their ruin is seen in their utter inability to save themselves. The love of Christ, that it may save sinners, must be deeper than their sin, more fathomless than their wretchedness. It is an ocean of love. Standing on the shore of this ocean, we can only exclaim, with admiring ecstacy, "Oh the depth!" Under the operation of this love the redeemed will be raised from the deep darkness of the grave, with bodies like their Lord's.

IV. *Height.* Another measurement remains to be considered. Because the love is deep, it raises the saved high. When delivered from condemnation and accepted in Christ, they are elevated. When exalted to the relation of children of God by regeneration and adoption, how high is their position! The love of Christ raises them to this elevation. They are raised so high that angels are appointed to serve them. Heb. i. 13. They will be raised to heaven and imparadised in the presence of God. They will appear before the throne in all the beauty of holiness. Eph. v. 25–27. As redeemed by blood, the blood of the loving Christ, they will have a higher distinction and a brighter glory than angels. When they reach the sublime altitudes of heaven, the height of their elevation will forever prove the height of Christ's love.

REMARKS.

I. Make the love of Christ your study.

II. Measure it as far as possible.

CHRIST'S LOVE FOR EVERY DISCIPLE.

. . . **Who loved me, and gave himself for me.—Gal. ii. 20.**

These words are taken from one of the most remarkable verses in the Holy Scriptures. We have the paradox of a crucified man, who lives in spite of his crucifixion; aye more, by means of his crucifixion. But observe, the crucifixion is with Christ—so effectually put to death that all the life in me is from Christ. Indeed, I no longer live, but Christ lives in me. He is the source of the life, and the life is maintained by faith. Paul thus expresses himself, and very naturally refers to the love of Christ. "Who loved me, and gave himself for me."

The subject to which I invite your attention is—

CHRIST'S LOVE FOR EVERY DISCIPLE.

It is very common for us to contemplate the love of Christ as embracing the myriads of the redeemed; and because they are numberless, we think of his love as so diffused that a very small portion of it is expended on us. Now I have chosen this text that I may, if possible, induce every Christian before me to say with Paul, "who loved *me*." Forget everybody else. Forget patriarchs, prophets, apostles, and all the hosts of martyrs. Repeat the text with the most intense personality of application: "who loved me," *me*, ME. Consider this love—

I. *In connection with its date.* Fixing the proper date has much to do in aggrandizing the love. Did Christ begin to love you when you were born? If so, what follows? Obviously, that his death had no reference to you, for he died long before your birth. To date his love from your birth will not do. Nor will it do to date it from his advent, for that would make the advent purposeless; whereas it occurred in pursuance of purpose. Is the creation of the world the proper date? Plainly not; for we are told that all things were created by Christ and for him. Then it follows that the earth was made for him—made that he might die on it; nor can his death be severed from his love. There was the purpose to make the earth before it was made, and his love, inseparable from his death, was equally inseparable from his purpose—his purpose to make the earth and to die on it. The date of the love was before creation, as we may learn from 2 Tim. i. 9; Titus i. 2. Any period antecedent to creation is equivalent to *from eternity.* Here is the proper date. Jer. xxxi. 3. Now you may say, Who loved me from eternity; loved me before a star twinkled in the diadem of night, or the sun measured the day; before there was any day or any night. You may say, Christ loved *me* through the long cycles of a past eternity. Does it seem incredible? Every Christian may say with Paul, "Who loved me, and gave himself for me."

II. *In connection with the unworthiness of its object.* I use object in the singular that you may not forget the *me* of the text. While the love of Christ fixed its regards on you personally, it of necessity contemplated you as unworthy; for its great manifestation, as we shall see, recognizes your unworthiness and your ruin. Your unworthiness rendered necessary what Christ did to save you. It originated the necessity of your salvation. Think of your unworthiness. Think of yourself as condemned, depraved, hostile to the Divine Government. You may say, the law condemned me, sin corrupted me, Christ regarded me as his enemy. Still he loved me in spite of my unworthiness. He exercised toward me the love of benevolence, and this love looked to such a change in my character as would make possible the love of complacency. What words! He loved me. Think of this love in connection with your unworthiness. Human love is based on real or imaginary worthiness. You see how peculiar is Christ's love to you. Do you say, surely there is some mistake? Christ could not love one so unworthy. Well, consider his love—

III. *In connection with the proof of it.* What says the text? "Gave himself for me." What a gift! This gift was freely bestowed. There was no compulsion. Christ had the sovereign disposal of himself, as we see in John x. 18. He had, therefore, the disposal of all things. He could have given planets, stars, worlds, suns, for you, but he did not. He gave *himself.* You can say this, my brother, my sister, "gave himself for *me.*" The words "for me" indicate that Christ gave himself thus:

1. *As my substitute.* For me, in place of me, as many Scriptures teach. You are ready to say, this is the basis of my hope, that Jesus took my place in law, and died in my

stead. Gal. iii. 13; 1 Peter iii. 18. Blessed doctrine of substitution!

2. *For my benefit.* This follows: If Christ died in my place, he died for my benefit. There is no saving benefit in his death unless he died as a substitute; but having died as a substitute, there is infinite benefit accruing from his death. You may say, Christian, he gave himself for my benefit, and the benefit includes all that is meant by salvation.

REMARKS.

I. Surely you belong to Christ.

II. Live for him—to his glory.

ALL FULLNESS IN CHRIST.

For it pleased the Father that in him shonld all fullness dwell.—Col. i. 19.

I. *Fullness of light to illuminate.*

II. *Fullness of atoning merit to justify.*

III. *Fullness of sanctifying virtue to cleanse from sin.*

IV. *Fullness of strength to sustain his disciples.*

V. *Fullness of life to make his followers live forever.*

REMARKS.

I. Is this complete Saviour yours?

II. Those who partake of his fullness will dwell with him in heaven.

III. If you share not in his fullness your wants can never be supplied.

THE ATONEMENT OF CHRIST, WITH ITS EXPERIMENTAL AND PRACTICAL INFLUENCES.

Who his own self bare our sins in his own body on the tree, that we being dead to sins, should live unto righteousness.—1 Peter ii. 24.

The atonement of Christ may be regarded as the founda

tion of the gospel. If this foundation can be overturned, the whole superstructure of Christianity falls, and buries in its ruins the hopes of all the saints. The doctrine of atonement is the central truth in theology, to which all other truths sustain a vital relation.

Under the inspiration of the text, I now discuss—

THE ATONEMENT OF CHRIST, WITH ITS EXPERIMENTAL AND PRACTICAL INFLUENCES.

I. *The atonement of Christ.* The word is used but once in the New Testament. Rom. v. 11. There it has its old meaning of reconciliation. In theological literature, it means expiation of sin by the obedience and death of Christ. It is a reparation of the dishonor inflicted on the divine law by sin. It is a satisfaction rendered to the justice of God. It is is a measure adopted in the administration of the Divine Government instead of the execution of the penalty of the law on personal transgressors, a measure supplying an honorable basis for the exercise of pardoning mercy. Let us see if such a measure is not found in the death of Christ. What says the text? "He bare our sins." To bear sin or iniquity, is a phrase of frequent occurrence in the Old Testament. It means to endure the penalty due to sin. This is taught in Lev. v. 1. The man referred to was to bear the consequences of his iniquity. We can now understand what is meant by Christ's bearing our iniquity. Isa. liii. 6, 12; Heb. ix. 28. These passages do not teach that Christ became personally guilty. Guilty, as we now use the word, implies personal criminality. Christ could not be guilty in this sense. There was no transfer of moral character from those he died for to him. 1 Peter iii. 18. This was impossible. Jesus bore our iniquity in the sense of bearing its consequences. In assuming our place in law, he agreed to meet the claims of law against us. To do this he must suffer for our sins, on account of our sins. He must suffer in our stead. His sufferings must be substituted for what we deserved to suffer. Taking our place he bore the consequences of our sins. He met our legal responsibilities. This was the only way in which he could bear our sins, for he could not personally become a sinner. He was made under the law to redeem those under the law. The Lawgiver laid on him the iniquity of us all. In bearing that iniquity, in suffering on the cross what we deserved to suffer, Jesus made atonement. His death was a governmental equivalent, and more than an equivalent, for the infliction of the curse of the law on sinners themselves. The law was not only magnified, but glorified. Jesus is the Lamb of God. The sacrifices of the law could not take away sins. There was a lack of dignity in the victims offered, and a lack of value in their blood. In Christ there was a victim of suitable dignity, and there was blood of the requisite atoning value. We see the doctrine of atonement set forth in the fact that Christ bore our sins on the cross.

II. *Influences of the atonement.* This great measure was designed to produce effects. It has such influence on the Divine Government as to render its honor harmonious with the salvation of sinners. It is the basis of a sinner's acceptance with God. In the text two other influences of the atonement are named. I shall call them—

1. *Experimental.* This effect of the atonement is referred to in the text by the words "being dead to sins." It is through the atonement that the agency of the Holy Spirit is secured, by which the heart is changed. In this change death to sin occurs. In the phrase "dead to sin," there seems to be a reference to the unity of sin—sin in the mass. "Dead to sins," refers rather to sin in its fearful diversity of operation and form. What is death to sins? The word translated 'being dead," means to be away from, separated from. In death to sins the power of sin is broken and the love of sin is

destroyed. There is a moral separation from sin in regeneration, as there is a legal, judicial separation from it in justification. It is not strange that there is a connection between the atonement and death to sin; for the atonement shows most clearly the evil of sin. Where else do we have such a view of sin? Not in the banishment of rebel angels, not in the exile from Eden, not in the ravages of death, not in the miseries of hell. Figuratively, we are dead to that which has no influence over us. He over whom worldly honor has no influence is dead to worldly honor. Believers in Christ are not under the dominion of sin, for they are dead to it. This death results from the atonement of Christ in its experimental influence and power on the heart. The atonement has no saving value for any man apart from its experimental effect, as seen in death to sin.

2. *Practical.* That the atonement has a practical influence is indicated by the words "should live unto righteousness." The experimental is followed by the practical; that is to say, those who die to sin live unto righteousness. To live unto righteousness is to live righteously. No sooner does death to sin occur than the life to righteousness begins. The life springs from the death. Death to sin involves hatred of sin and consequent love of holiness. The hatred and the love, acting conjointly, lead to a righteous life. The evil tree having been made good, its fruit is good. The heart controls the life. When regeneration creates a right state of heart the life is conformed to principles of righteousness. It is therefore written that we are "created in Christ Jesus unto good works." Eph. ii. 10. It is also written that "the grace of God that bringeth salvation hath appeared to all men, teaching us that denying ungodliness and worldly lusts, we should live soberly, righteously, and godly, in this present world." Titus ii. 11, 12. Thus the atonement in its saving influences has to do with the life as well as with the heart.

REMARKS.

I. While the atonement of Christ is the great doctrine of Christianity, it creates a rich experience and leads to a correct practice.

II. Those only are savingly benefited by the atonement who die to sin and live to righteousness.

FOR JESUS' SAKE.

. . . **For Jesus' sake.—2 Cor. iv. 5.**

No words are more common than these. They are used at the close of most public prayers, and doubtless of private prayers also. As they are so common, there is danger lest we forget their import. They are words of great significance and power. He who understands them, as used in the Scriptures, is no mean theologian; for all the blessings of salvation on earth and in heaven have a sacred connection with Jesus, and are bestowed for his sake. The text and theme will be identical.

FOR JESUS' SAKE.

To elucidate the sacred topic let us consider it—

I. *As suggesting the ground of acceptance with God.* If we wish to learn man's natural condition before God, we need only to read Rom. iii. 10–19. Sinners, because of their sins, are under the wrath of God. This wrath is said to come on them. Eph. v. 6. It abides on them. John iii. 36. This is the opposite of a state of acceptance with God. How can sinners be accepted? The difficulty is not with holy, but with unholy beings. Holiness is a passport of acceptance with God in any world. Sin is the great obstruction to acceptance. Nothing sinners can do or suffer will procure their acceptance with God. If accepted at all, it must be in the Beloved, and Jesus is the Beloved. To be accepted there must be forgiveness and reconciliation, and they both come through Christ. Eph. iv. 32; Col. i. 21, 22. They come through him alone. Acts iv. 12. He himself said, "No man cometh to the Father but by me." John xiv. 6. For the sake of what Jesus has done and suffered, those who believe in him are received into a state of favor with God. This great blessing of salvation is conferred in recognition of Jesus' merit.

II. *As furnishing an efficacious plea in prayer.* As there are no reasons in ourselves why we should be saved, so there are no reasons in ourselves why our prayers should be heard. Alas, for the man who expects his prayers to be heard for his own sake! We have no credit with God, no spiritual deposits, no resources of merit, on which to draw. How, then, are our prayers to avail? Only for Jesus' sake. This we learn from Rom. viii. 32; 1 John ii. 2. It is in connection with his Son that God freely gives us all things. Jesus is our Advocate. He is the Righteous, though he pleads for sinners The presence of an unrighteous advocate could not be tolerated in the court of heaven. Jesus has all the qualifications of a successful Advocate. He is able to present a valid reason why the prayers offered in his name should be granted. The reason is in his mediation. The resources of his mediatorial merit are exhaustless. The plea, "for Jesus' sake," avails with God. In consideration of what Jesus is, and of what he has done, God not only can hear prayer, but he delights to hear it. He loves to honor his Son by bestowing blessings for his sake. Surely the words, "for Jesus' sake," are suggestive of an efficacious plea in prayer. We must approach God with the Mediator's blood on our souls, and his name on our lips. God hears prayer only for Jesus' sake.

III. *As supplying a motive of exhaustless power.* There is no duty to the performance of which the words, "for Jesus' sake," do not prompt. Take the threefold duty of love—love to God—love to Christians—and love to impenitent sinners. Read John iii. 16, and you see that the gift of his Son furnishes the strongest reason why we should love God. There are other reasons, but this is the grandest, the sublimest. As to Christian love, see John xv 12; Eph. iv. 32. Christians are to love one another for Jesus' sake. This only is Christian love. The motive to exercise it is one of exhaustless power. Jesus died for your fellow-Christian, as well as for yourself. As to impenitent sinners; when we think that Jesus died for them, thus showing his love, we love them for his sake. You may say that some of them are repulsive. This may be; but Jesus loved them, and you should love them for his sake. It cannot be beneath you to love what Jesus loved. It cannot be a condescension to labor for the salvation of those for whom Christ died. Take with you the words, "for Jesus' sake," when you go forth to labor for souls. Repeat these words when you think of your talents, your time, your property, your influence, your everything. Feel the power of these words, and there will be self-sacrificing consecration to Christ. Think of them supplying a motive to bear trials. These trials may come for Jesus' sake; and they can be borne for his sake when they would be borne for no other reason. They may be borne with pleasure. 2 Cor. xii. 10. It would be easy to revile when we are reviled, but a remembrance of the words, "for Jesus' sake," will prevent it. See what Stephen said, when dying: "Lord, lay not this sin to their charge." Acts vii. 60.

IV. *As securing admittance into heaven.* Jesus is the Way to heaven—the Way, the Truth, and the Life. Earth's distant population can reach the bright mansions of glory through Christ alone. The celestial gates will open wide for the entrance of those who have been washed in the blood of the Lamb. The language of the saved is recorded in Rev.

v. 9: "Thou wast slain, and hast redeemed us to God by thy blood out of every kindred, and tongue, and people, and nation." We have precious words, too, in Rev. vii. 14–17. Blessed are those whom the Lamb shall lead to fountains of living water, and from whose eyes God shall wipe all tears.

ALL THINGS GIVEN BY THE FATHER TO THE SON.

The Father loveth the Son, and hath given all things into his hand. —John iii. 35.

Jealousy is a contemptible feeling; and, strange to say, it showed itself among the disciples of John the Baptist toward the Lord Jesus. They were troubled on account of John's waning popularity and the increasing fame of Christ. They went to John with their complaint (verse 26). He let them know that the very thing which troubled them delighted him. He exulted in Christ's superiority. Refer to verses 30, 31, 34. The Spirit is given to the Son in unmeasured abundance. Jewish kings and priests were anointed with oil; Christ was anointed with the Spirit. The reason of this is given in the text. The Father loveth the Son. The topic that will now engage our thoughts is this:

ALL THINGS GIVEN BY THE FATHER TO THE SON.

Notice—

I. *The Father's love for the Son.* The unity of God is prominent among the teachings of the Bible. There is but one God. This one God, however, has revealed himself in a threefold personality—as Father, Son, Spirit. There is such a distinction of persons, or subsistences, as justifies the Father in designating himself to say *I*, in addressing the Son to say *Thou*, and in referring to the Spirit to say *He*. This is to us incomprehensible. We accept it as true because inspiration declares it. When Jesus is called the Son of man, his relation to man is taught; when he is termed the Son of God, his relation to God is taught. God sent his Son into the world, and he was therefore his Son before he was sent. This is enough for us to know. The Father loves the Son. This we learn from the Old Testament and the New. Isa. xlii. 1; Matt. iii. 17; Col. i. 13. There is such a distinction between the Father and the Son that the former loves the latter—loved him before his incarnation—loved him as divine—and loves him since his incarnation as the Christ, the Mediator. There is one Scripture which intimates that he loves him more on account of his work of mediation. John x. 17. The love is as intense as a Being of infinite powers can feel toward an object of infinite loveliness. No language can describe this love, no mind can conceive its strength. God's love of the world, as seen in the gift of his Son, is unspeakably great, because of his antecedent love for his Son.

II. *The Father has given all things into the hand of his Son.* He has done this because of his love. Love for his Son has induced the surrender of all things into his hand. We learn from Matt. xxviii. 18, that "all power," or rather, authority, is given to Christ. The careful reader of the Scriptures will observe that the second person in the Godhead is said to exercise two kinds of power—that is to say, underived power and delegated power. The former was exerted in creation (John i. 3), the latter is mediatorial. It has been given to Christ as Mediator; for as Mediator he acts in subordination to the Father and does his will. John vi. 38; Heb. x. 5–7. That there is a delegation of power, authority, to Christ, we see, not only from the text, but from Psalm ii. 6; Matt xi. 27; John xvii. 2; Phil. ii. 9–11. Speaking after the manner of men, we may say that the administration of the Divine Government has been transferred from the hands of God absolute to the hands of the Incarnate Mediator. This transfer is so complete that God has nothing to do with men independently of the Mediator, and men have nothing to do with God out of Christ; for he is in Christ reconciling the world unto himself. Men may object that Jesus administers the Divine Government, but they cannot have it otherwise. He is doing so in pursuance of a decree, for the execution of which all the resources of omnipotence are pledged. But observe—

All things are given into Christ's hands. Let us contemplate these "all things" as follows:

1. *All things pertaining to providence.* Jesus rules in the realm of providence. Kingdoms and empires rise and flourish, if it is his pleasure; they fall and perish under his displeasure. He is the Head over all things to the church; that is, for the benefit of his church, redeemed by his blood. He makes the wrath of man to praise him. He reigns supremely in the empire of providence.

2. *All things pertaining to grace.* It was given into his hand to open the channel for the consistent outflow of the stream of grace from the fountain of love into the parched deserts of sin. Grace reached man through Christ. Rom. v 21. The cross is the monument of grace. Jesus is the Author of salvation, and salvation is of grace. He dispenses grace. John iv. 10, 14; Acts xv. 11. No soul is saved that does not receive grace through Christ. The treasures of grace are at his disposal. He fully earned, by his death, the right to dispense them.

3. *All things pertaining to glory.* Jesus exercises the right to appoint for his followers a place in heaven. Luke xxii. 29; John xiv. 2, 3. He gives his disciples eternal life. John x. 28; xiv. 19; xvii. 2; Jude 21. He has the great boon of eternal life at his disposal. He will say who shall inherit the kingdom of heaven. Matt. xxv. 34. It is given to him to clothe the resurrection body with *glory* brighter than the sun.

4. *All things pertaining to the destiny of the wicked.* He

must reign till he puts all enemies under his feet. The judgment seat is *his*. He will pronounce its decisions on the ungodly. Matt. xxv. 41. It will be fearful for sinners to be judged by the man of Calvary; but their sentence will be pronounced by him. He who on the throne of grace says to them, "Come unto me," will on the throne of judgment say, "Depart from me." Truly all things are in the hands of Christ.

REMARKS.

I. It is very safe to trust in Jesus.

II. It is utterly ruinous to reject him.

GOD SEEING THE BLOOD, PASSES OVER.

And when I see the blood, I will pass over you.—Ex. xii. 13.

The time for Israel's deliverance had come. The oppressions of the Egyptians were to cease. There was to be mourning from one end of Egypt to the other. The first-born in every family was to be smitten by the hand of the Lord. This was done at midnight. Verses 29, 30. What a calamity! But the Israelites were safe. Why? The divine arrangement was for the blood of a lamb, killed in each family, to be applied to the lintels and door-posts of each house. Paul tells us that Christ our Passover has been sacrificed for us You see, therefore, that the paschal lamb was typical. I trust we shall learn some spiritual lessons while we fix our contemplations on this topic:

GOD SEEING THE BLOOD, PASSES OVER.

I invite your attention to—

I. *The Blood.* Consider the blood of the type. The lamb was to be perfect and without blemish. Being the symbol of innocence, its blood was regarded as precious. It was shed, too, by God's appointment. Nothing was done in the matter without the divine sanction. The deliverance was to be wrought in God's own way. The Antitype was divinely appointed. John i. 29; vi. 27; Heb. x. 7. Jesus not only came into the world voluntarily, but he came in pursuance of the purpose and plan of the Father. His blood was shed according to the will of God, and has all the value which divine sanction can confer. It is evident, however, that divine appointment, though indispensable, is not sufficient of itself to give the requisite worth to sacrificial blood. This we learn from what is said in the Epistle to the Hebrews about the inefficacy of animal sacrifices. There was a want of dignity and worth in the victims slain under the Mosaic law. Hence the constant repetition of the sacrifices. When Christ, the antitype came, there was a suitable victim, whose blood was of infinite value. Here the analogy between the blood of the type and of the antitype utterly fails. Why was the blood of Jesus possessed of such value? Because it was the blood of the Christ. Who is the Christ? He is the God-man. I enter not into the question whether divinity could or did suffer when Jesus died. I assume it as unquestionably true that divinity imparted infinite worth to the atoning blood of the cross. It is precious blood. It is the blood of a spiritual and eternal redemption.

II. *The sight of the blood.* "When I see the blood, I will pass over." It was not enough for the blood of the paschal lamb to be shed and carefully preserved, or even put anywhere except on the lintels and door-posts. Suppose any family of Israel had sprinkled the blood on the floor, or on the sides of the house, it would have afforded no protection, for it would not have been the symbol of deliverance. It must be where God commanded it to be. The symbolic importance of the blood was in its application. So of the blood of the Lamb of God. Its saving efficacy is confined to its application. Its intrinsic worth is infinite, but its virtue to save reaches those only who believe. You may see this truth forcibly illustrated in Mark v. 30–34. The gospel is "the power of God unto salvation to every one that believeth." "The righteousness of God is by faith of Jesus Christ unto all and upon all them that believe." Rom. i. 16; iii. 22. There is, if I may so say, an application of Christ's justifying blood the moment a sinner believes in him, and afterward there are continuous applications of his cleansing, sanctifying blood. Perhaps it is better to say, that his blood in its justifying merit and sanctifying virtue is applied. God sees it. You may not. The great thing is for God to see it. He sees it if it is applied, otherwise not.

III. *The result which follows the sight of the blood.* "I will pass over you." Several millions of Israelites were saved from temporal destruction through the blood of the paschal lamb. The blood was the symbol of their deliverance. God passed over and left them in safety. So of spiritual redemption through the blood of Christ. God seeth blood on his redeemed ones and passes over them. The sacred mark guarantees their rescue from danger. They are safe. There is the desponding Christian who says: "I am so guilty, how can I be passed over?" God says: "When I see the blood, I will pass over you." The weak believer says: "My sins rise like mountains." God says: "When I see the blood, I will pass over you." The humble saint says: "I am so unworthy." God says: "I do not look at your unworthiness, but at the blood." The trembling disciple exclaims: "My heart is so polluted, it is my constant trouble." God says: "When I see the blood, I will pass over you." "I have fightings without and fears within," cries another. God says: "When I see the blood, I will pass over you." Here comes the tremulous voice of one who says: "I see the darkness of death and the terrors of judgment before me, and my heart sinks." God says: "When I see the blood, I will pass over you." The blood will be a sure protection, here and hereafter. *Passover*, PASSOVER, PASSOVER.

REMARKS.

I. It is not enough that Jesus died.
II. His blood must be applied.
III. Does God see this blood on you?
IV. Woe to those who trifle with the blood of the cross.

THE EMPTY GRAVE OF JESUS.

Come, see the place where the Lord lay.—Matt. xxviii. 6.

Whether a place is occupied or vacant is sometimes a matter of great significance. The occupancy or the abdication of a throne has involved the interests of millions. The operations of war furnish many instances of the wisdom or folly of holding or abandoning places. At times, the fact that a place is held is very suggestive; at other times, that a place is vacated is more suggestive. Of all the unoccupied places in the universe I know of none teaching lessons so important as the empty grave of Jesus. That grave had possession of his body from the day of crucifixion to the first day of the next week; but from then till now it has been empty. The angel said to the anxious women, "Come, see the place where the Lord lay"—where he did lie—not there now. Let us mentally approach and see where the Lord was once lying. My theme is—

THE EMPTY GRAVE OF JESUS.

From its emptiness we may learn such lessons as these:

I. *That he is the Christ.* He affirmed during his ministry that he was the Messiah, the Son of God. See John iv. 25, 26; and ix. 35-37. On his mock-trial before the Jewish

Council, the high priest put him on his oath, saying: "I adjure thee by the living God, tell us whether thou be the Christ." Matt. xxvi. 63, 64. How majestic his answer! The Jews said he was an impostor, and their highest court pronounced him a blasphemer. The issue was made, he affirming and his enemies denying his divine Sonship. When he was nailed to the cross the Jews were confirmed in their view. Mark xv. 31, 32. He did not come down from the cross. He died, was buried, and the hopes of the disciples were buried with him. How still he lies in the sepulchre! But he has said that he would rise. His resurrection is ascribed to himself, and also to his Father. If we consider him as rising by his own power, there is a demonstration of his Messiahship; and if we contemplate him as raised by the Father, there is not only a demonstration, but an indorsement of his Messiahship. Rom. i. 4. Would God indorse the character of an impostor? Infinitely impossible. A voice, therefore, comes out of the empty grave of Jesus, and proclaims in trumpet tones that he is the Christ. There would be no such voice if the grave was not empty. On the supposition that Jesus of Nazareth was an impostor, it was impossible for him to rise from the dead; on the supposition that he was the Christ, it was impossible for him not to rise.

II. *The all-sufficiency and the acceptance of his atoning sacrifice.* His sacrifice was necessary to the removal of legal obstacles out of the way of man's salvation. The law of God had been transgressed and justice had been offended. Christ, "the man of sorrows," and the victim of Calvary, undertook to satisfy law and justice by his obedience and death. Satisfaction is the central idea in atonement, and if satisfaction had not been rendered, there would have been no resurrection of Christ. Law and justice would have protested against it forever. The words of the text would never have been heard. The grave would not have become an empty one. The emptiness of the grave, therefore, shows the competency of Christ's atoning sacrifice to effect the purposes for which it was made. The grave left without its illustrious Occupant says to more worlds than this, that the sacrifice of Jesus was all-sufficient, and was accepted by the Lawgiver—was to him "a sweet-smelling savor." Eph. v. 2.

III. *That it is safe to trust in him for salvation.* Who could trust in him if his grave were not empty? On this hypothesis there would be a perfect absence of the crowning proof of his Messiahship and of the all-sufficiency and the acceptance of his atoning sacrifice. With his empty grave before us, we know who he is, and what he has done. Hence we are sure that it is safe to trust in him for salvation. Having risen from the dead, he is evermore alive and able to superintend the interests committed to his care. Rom. v. 10; Heb. vii. 25. The empty grave of Jesus tells of the safety of trusting in him. Paul knew this. 2 Tim. i. 12. We trust in a living Saviour, who was dead, but is not dead now; whose grave was once occupied, but is empty now. Nothing is safer than trusting Christ, and the safety is indicated by his empty grave.

IV. *That his followers will rise as certainly as he rose.* "The last Adam," as well as the first, is a representative character, and he never acted more representatively than in rising from the dead. He is called "the first-fruits of them that slept." The after-fruits must come. Jesus is the resurrection and the life. The redemption of which he is the Author is so complete that it provides for the salvation of the body as well as the soul. The resurrection will be a wondrous epoch in the history of the saints. Paul calls it "the adoption, to wit, the redemption of our body." Rom. viii. 23. It is the last, the *public* act of adoption. The first act was a private matter between God and the soul; the last will have all possible publicity. The empty grave of Jesus is prophetic of the emptiness of the graves of all his followers. Wherever their graves may be, whether in the earth or in the sea, they are destined to become empty. Jesus will never see of the travail of his soul so as to be satisfied till he sees all the redeemed raised from the dead with bodies like his own. How majestic are the words recorded in Phil. iii. 21! The empty grave of Jesus speaks of the resurrection of all his followers and amply guarantees it.

REMARKS.

I. Study these lessons more earnestly and devoutly.

II. The more thoroughly they are understood, the greater the joy of the saints.

III. Let sinners remember that Jesus lives to save all willing to be saved by him.

JESUS DELIVERS FROM WRATH.

And to wait for his Son from heaven, whom he raised from the dead, even Jesus, who delivered us from the wrath to come.—1 Thess. i. 10.

It is well for Christians to think of the wrath referred to in the text, for they have been delivered from it, and should feel the devoutest gratitude to their Deliverer. The impenitent ought to consider this wrath, for they are exposed to it, and must be saved from it, or perish forever.

Let us contemplate the proposition that—

JESUS DELIVERS FROM WRATH.

It is proper to notice—

I. *Characteristics of this wrath.*

Let us notice the following:

1. *It is the wrath of God.* We must not think God's wrath like turbulent passion in man. It is not. The wrath of God

s his righteous and holy indignation against sin. Sin is the disturber of the moral harmony of the universe. It is a violation of justice and holiness. It must therefore excite in the divine mind intense abhorrence and indignation. This wrath of God is revealed from heaven. Rom. i. 18.

2. *It is due to sinners.* Their sins have provoked it, and will call for the most awful displays of its power. Its manifestations will be regulated by the deserts of sinners.

3. *It is without mixture of mercy.* In this life, however great afflictions and trials may be, there are always mercies intermingled, there are circumstances of mitigation. Not so with regard to the wrath of God in the world to come. There will be no mixture, no manifestation of mercy.

4. *It is endless wrath.* The text speaks of wrath to come. What words! When myriads of ages, more numerous than the stars, shall have passed away, it will still be wrath to come! It will always be wrath to come.

II. *Jesus has delivered believers from this wrath.* This is the delightful teaching of the text. Deliverance was possible only through his perfect mediatorial work.

1. *His atonement supplies the basis for the deliverance.* He speaks in the hearing of the universe, saying, concerning the believer, "Deliver him from going down to the pit: I have found a ransom." Job xxxiii. 24. His obedience and blood so magnified the law as to provide for a consistent remission of its penalty.

2. *This deliverance is through faith in Christ.* Faith makes the believer one with Christ and secures the imputation of his righteousness. Then he can say, with triumphant defiance, "Who shall lay anything to my charge?"

3. *The deliverance involves all that is meant by salvation.* Yes, every thing included in salvation on earth and in heaven. Deliverance from the wrath to come is followed by a blissful initiation into the glory to come, which is eternal glory.

III. *Christians ought to live with reference to the second coming of Christ.*

1. *He will come again.* He has so said. Angels have repeated it. Apostles have reiterated it. His second coming is the greatest promise to his people yet to be fulfilled.

2. *Believers should assume an expectant attitude.* They should look for him and love his appearing. He will come, not as he first came, "to bear the sins of many," but "without sin unto salvation,"—to consummate salvation. The day of his coming will be earth's brightest day.

> Ye sinners, seek his grace,
> Whose wrath ye cannot bear;
> Fly to the shelter of his cross,
> And find salvation there.

CHRIST'S EXPECTANT ATTITUDE.

From henceforth expecting till his enemies be made his footstool.—Heb. x. 13.

We are all creatures of expectation. Whether satisfied with the present or not, we look for something in the future. There is the expectation of dread, and there is the expectation of desire. We fear and we hope. Angels expect. Fallen angels anticipate greater wretchedness, and holy angels expect an eternal continuance of their bliss. The feeling of expectation is not confined to men and angels. The Lord of angels and men is referred to in the text as expecting. Christ, having died, risen, and ascended, is seated at the right hand of God, in a state of serene and majestic expectation. "From henceforth expecting." The subject I present for your contemplation is—

CHRIST'S EXPECTANT ATTITUDE.

The verse preceding the text indicates that the Redeemer's expectation bears date from the acceptance of his one sacrifice, the proof of which acceptance is seen in his being at the right hand of God. Let us consider—

I. *Christ has enemies.* We are almost ready to say, Who would expect this? Especially, who would suppose that these enemies include men? Can men be his enemies, in view of the amazing facts that he took on him their nature? that he died for their salvation? and that he offers them mercy? But if so, will not his exaltation to the right hand of God overcome their enmity and induce cheerful submission to him? Alas, none of these things removes their enmity. You may say that Christ has friends in the world. Yes, but he has never had a friend on earth till he first subdued an enemy. We see his enemies among all classes, in high places and low places. Even among his professed friends there are now, as in apostolic times, "enemies of the cross." Well may his friends, like Paul, weep over the sad fact. Death is called "the last enemy." 1 Cor. xv. 26. He is the progeny of sin. Rom. v. 12. Death reigns and has reigned from Adam till now. He shuts up all his subjects in the prison-house of the grave. While the grave has tenants there will be proof that "the last enemy" is not subdued. I may say, however, that—

II. *Christ's enemies will all be subdued.* This we are told in various places. Psalm cx. 1; Matt. xx. 42–45; 1 Cor. xv. 25. Thus the teaching of the text is fortified. As to Christ's human enemies, it is to be said that they will be subdued by the sceptre of his grace or by the sceptre of his justice. These are the two methods of subjugation. Let us consider them.

1. *Sceptre of grace.* All who become Christians bow to this sceptre. To these there is reference in Psalm cx. 3—"Willing in the day of thy power." The day of Christ's power is when men are made willing to be saved. No man is naturally willing to be saved by Christ. All men are willing to be saved on terms of their own, but not on Christ's

terms. Those only accept who are convinced of sin and feel their guilty, ruined condition. They gladly bow to the sceptre of grace. They become Christ's loyal subjects. Changed from enemies, they are bound to him by the ties of everlasting friendship and love.

2. *Sceptre of justice.* Those who do not bow to the golden sceptre of grace, must bow to the iron sceptre of justice. This is the dreadful alternative. How much is submitted to the option of men! Life and death are set before them. They are called on to choose life. What did Jesus say to the Jews? Matt. xxiii. 37; John v. 40. Here we see unwillingness to bow to the sceptre of grace—a refusal to be saved by Christ. The other method of subjugation must be resorted to—

His mercy knows the appointed bound,
And yields to justice there.

When it is said that Christ's enemies will be made his *footstool,* two ideas are conveyed, one of complete subjugation, the other of complete degradation. The latter is responsive to the "everlasting contempt," referred to in Daniel xii. 2.

3. *Death will be abolished.* This will be done by means of the resurrection. Death can do his work only in that which is mortal; but the resurrection will stamp that which is mortal with immorality. What then can death do? There will be no material to work upon, and by a blessed necessity death will die. Then the Redeemer's conquest will be complete; and this is Paul's argument in 1 Cor. xv. 26. Hence the Common Version does the argument great injustice, and the Revised Version strangely indorses the injustice; for it only substitutes *abolished* for destroyed. When it is said, "The last enemy that shall be destroyed (or, *abolished*) is death," nothing is said concerning the completeness of the Redeemer's triumph; for other enemies may remain undestroyed. But a correct translation, namely, "Death, the last enemy, shall be de-

stroyed," makes the matter entirely plain. The completeness of Christ's triumph is brought out; for no enemy remains after the last enemy is destroyed. All Christ's foes are to be subdued.

III. *Christ's expectant attitude.* "Expecting till his enemies be made his footstool." You will observe that he is to wait in expectation till this is done. Then he is to deliver his mediatorial kingdom to God the Father, that God in his threefold unity may be all in all. 1 Cor. xv. 24. The idea seems to be that for the accomplishment of certain purposes the mediatorial kingdom of Christ was established; and when these objects are accomplished the kingdom is to be surrendered to the Father, so as to merge into the universal and eternal kingdom of God. Christ is expecting that epoch of the universe. His expectation is based on the promise of the Father, his God and our God. We are therefore told that "God has highly exalted him, and given him a name which is above every name: that at the name of Jesus every knee should bow, of things in heaven, and things in earth, and things under the earth; and that every tongue should confess that Jesus Christ is Lord, to the glory of God the Father. Phil. ii. 9–11. The great and glorious day when every knee shall bow and every tongue confess to Jesus the Nazarene, will surely come. Christ is sitting in majestic repose at the right hand of God, and waiting for the day to come. His attitude is expectant. He expects the Father to perform his promise, overturning kingdoms and empires that antagonize his plans, and taking all the centuries necessary so to do what he has said, as to give the universe the most luminous exhibition of the divine glory. "From henceforth expecting till his enemies be made his footstool."

REMARKS.

I. The best interests of every rational creature are involved in loyaltv to Christ.

II. Blessed are the obedient subjects of his grace.

III. Terrible will be the doom of his enemies who fall under the stroke of his justice.

THE EXCELLENCE OF THE GOSPEL.

How beautiful are the feet of them that preach the gospel of peace, and bring glad tidings of good things!—Romans x. 15.

In a preceding verse we have the general proposition, "For whosoever shall call on the name of the Lord shall be saved." This proposition brings out an admirable specimen of interrogative logic. Four questions are asked, and each question conveys a negative idea more forcibly than would a positive statement. "How then shall they call on him in whom they have not believed?" As if the apostle had said, It is impossible. So of the other questions. Having referred to preachers as messengers of salvation, Paul utters the words of the text, quoted substantially from Isa. lii. 7.

The theme I extract is this:

THE EXCELLENCE OF THE GOSPEL.

This excellence is seen in three things:

I. *The feet of the messengers of the gospel are beautiful.* This, of course, is not to be understood literally. I will try to make the matter plain. If in this generation you are in a telegraph office, waiting for a welcome message, the click of the instrument would be sweeter to you than music. Why? Not in itself, surely, but on account of the message. Go back sixty years ago, to the time of stage-coaches carrying the mails, and you can fancy that the sound of the rolling wheels was melody to the man expecting a letter with news so welcome and important as to throw a halo of prosperity on all his future career. Now transport yourselves to the days of Isaiah, from whom Paul, quotes. Then men ran to carry messages. See 2 Sam. xviii. 19, 21, 24–26. Isaiah says: "How beautiful upon the mountains are the feet." The feet, the means by which the messengers ran, would first be seen on the higher elevations. These feet would be beautiful, not in themselves, but on account of the welcome message they were bearing. You now see the meaning of the word "beautiful," as applied to the messengers of salvation. It indicates the excellence, the preciousness of their message. This message is the gospel.

II. *It is the gospel of peace.* This is the teaching of the text. That the gospel is the gospel of peace, is a strong proof of its excellence. We may consider it as announcing—

1. *Peace with God.* Ever since the fall, God and men have been at variance. That great disaster broke up harmony and fellowship between the Creator and the creature. It alienated man from God. Man is God's enemy, and is under his displeasure. God has a controversy with man. The two parties, God and man, being at variance, there must be a change in one or both before there can be peace. But God cannot change. The change, then, must occur in man. God, however, first proposes overtures of reconciliation. 2 Cor. v. 18–20. Wonderful overtures! God in Christ reconciling the world to himself! The plan is of divine origin and infinitely marvelous. God gave his Son to die that his mercy might consistently reach and save the guilty. Therefore, sinners seeking pardon in Christ's name, find it. God preaches peace by Jesus Christ. Acts x. 36. Being justified by faith, we have peace with God. Rom. v. 1. The gospel proclaims this peace.

2. *Peace of conscience.* This is inseparably allied to peace with God. The reason is, that whatever removes the obstacles to peace with God removes those which hinder peace of conscience. Jesus says: "Come unto me." Matt. xi. 28. He

promises rest, and the rest implies release and repose from the accusations of conscience. In coming to Christ, the sinner finds his heart sprinkled from an evil conscience. The evil, or accusing conscience, becomes a good conscience, and baptism is its answer. 1 Peter iii. 21.

3. *Peace between man and man.* This is the spirit of the gospel. What did the angels sing? Luke ii. 13, 14. The gospel is the gospel of peace. The kingdom of God is peace. Rom. xiv. 17. The fruit of the Spirit is peace. Gal. v. 22. Jesus pronounces peace-makers blessed. Matt. v. 9. We are required to follow peace with all men. Heb. xii. 14. The gospel of peace is to be the means of establishing peace throughout the world. What says the sure word of prophecy? Isa. ii. 2–4. The time of universal peace will come, and I argue the excellence of the gospel because it is the gospel of peace.

III. *It is glad tidings of good things.* The tidings are glad; that is, they make those who hear and receive them glad. They are glad tidings because they proclaim good things, the best things that mortal ears ever heard. What are some of these good things? I may name a few of them:

1. *Remission of sins.* The gospel of peace announces the terms of the New Covenant, according to which God remembers the sins of the covenantees no more. Heb. viii. 12. Jesus, who when on earth said, "Son, daughter, thy sins are forgiven thee," intended his words to be prophetic of what he would do in all the centuries.

2. *Adoption into the family of God.* See Gal. iv. 4, 5; 1 John iii. 1, 2. This is a great transition, from the family of Satan into the family of God. Jesus is "the first-born among many brethren." The junior members of the family are adopted through the blood of the first-born.

3. *A glorious resurrection.* If it is among the bad things

that we must die and return to the dust, it is among the good things that we shall rise from the grave; and the gospel announces this good thing.

4. *Everlasting life.* This is the great promise. 1 John ii. 25; Rom. vi. 23. Truly the gospel, in proclaiming everlasting life as the portion of the saints, proclaims a good thing; a thing so good that it will require eternity to comprehend how good.

REMARKS.

I. We should highly prize the gospel for its excellence.

II. It reveals the only way of salvation.

III. To reject it is to incur all that is meant by "the second death."

REPENTANCE AND FAITH.

Testifying both to the Jews, and also to the Greeks, repentance toward God, and faith toward our Lord Jesus Christ.—Acts xx. 21.

When these words were spoken by Paul, all the tender sensibilities of his soul were excited. He was delivering his farewell counsels to the Ephesian elders. He appealed to them as witnesses of his apostolic fidelity in keeping back nothing that was profitable. Ver. 20. He was going to Jerusalem. Ver. 22. He did not count his life dear to himself. Ver. 24. Happy minister who, in leaving those among whom he has labored, can say: "I am pure from the blood of all men." Ver. 26. Paul's ministry in Ephesus continued three years, and during that period, repentance toward God and faith toward our Lord Jesus Christ were the prominent topics on which he dwelt. Let these direct our meditation to-day.

REPENTANCE AND FAITH.

I. *Repentance.* What is it? It is something *inward*, for its outward fruit is reformation of life. It has to do with the heart, the mind; and implies such a change of mind in regard to sin as involves sorrow. It is sorrow with respect to sin. All sorrow is not repentance. For example, when our friends die, we feel sorrow; or when a calamity befalls a nation, we mourn; but we do not repent. Repentance has reference to *personal* sin. It cannot, therefore, be performed by proxy. Let us consider—

1. *Repentance toward God.* What does this mean? It means repentance with respect to God. You will say that this needs explanation. So it does. Here is the explanation:

a. God is a Lawgiver.—He has enacted a law, holy,just and good. Of this law sin is the trangression. Repentance, therefore, has reference to the fact that the Lawgiver has been sinned against in the violation of his law. It looks to sin rather than to its consequences. It involves a vindication of the Lawgiver and an approval of his law. By the law is the knowledge of sin. The repenting sinner sees the evil of sin as committed against God. Psalm li. 4; Dan. ix. 8; Luke xv. 18.

b. Hatred of sin as opposed to God. If in repentance there is an approval of God's law, there must be hatred of that which is contrary to it. Sin is that thing. Hence hatred of sin is inseparable from repentance. There is no repentance without it. The penitent hates and loathes himself on account of it. Job. xlii. 6.

c. Sorrow for sin as against God. It is against his nature, his will, his law, his government, his grace. It is altogether against him. From proper views of sin as a thing against God, sorrow results as inevitably as light and heat from the sun. Sorrow is the central element in repentance. This we may learn from Matt. xi. 21. Sackcloth and ashes were the symbols of sorrow and mourning in ancient times.

d. A purpose to sin against God no longer. This purpose is formed in connection with the hatred and sorrow referred to. The purpose is inward; its execution is outward, leading to reformation of life.

e. *Self-despair of atoning for sin.* The repenting sinner knows to his grief that his sin has proved his ruin, and knows equally well that repentance is not expiation. He can look on the ruin his sin has wrought, but is powerless to repair the injury. There is a feeling of helpless self-despair. But the gospel connects repentance with remission of sins. Luke xxiv. 47. This brings me to the second point of the text, namely:

II. *Faith.* You will observe that while repentance is toward God, faith is toward Christ. Repentance has respect to God as Lawgiver, and faith has respect to Christ as Saviour.

1. *Faith is toward our Lord Jesus Christ.* This means that the Lord Jesus Christ is the object of faith. Faith embraces him. It is not merely the belief of propositions concerning Christ, but reliance on him as a personal Saviour. The belief of propositions amounts to nothing apart from personal trust in the Redeemer. Why Christ is presented in the gospel as the object of faith, appears from two considerations:

a. *He has satisfied the claims of the Lawgiver.* To do this cost him much. It cost him the assumption of human nature. John i. 14. It cost him a life of poverty and privation, of slander and persecution. It cost him the bitter sorrows of Gethsemane. It cost him the sacrificial surrender of his life on Calvary. By his obedience and death—for his obedience was unto death—he magnified and even glorified the law by meeting the claims of the Lawgiver. He so offered himself without spot to God that the Lawgiver can pardon the sins which in repentance are deplored as against God. Because Christ was set "forth as a propitiation," God can be "just, and the justifier of him that believeth in Jesus." It is easy to conceive of God as just and the Punisher of sin; but the mysterious, the blessed wonder is that he can be just and pardon sin. Do you not see that faith has respect to Christ as a Saviour, even as repentance has respect to God as Lawgiver? The repentance for sins against the Lawgiver leads the sinner to Christ as the Saviour for pardon and salvation. Repentance precedes faith, and faith follows by a blessed necessity.

b. Faith unites to Christ. To share in the saving benefits of Christ's work of mediation there must be union with him. There must be acceptance in the Beloved. The union is formed by faith, the acceptance is by means of faith. There is no merit in faith, but there is infinite merit in its object, the Lord Jesus Christ. Hence the connection between faith and salvation. I may illustrate this point by referring to the blind man whose sight was restored, and to whom Jesus said, "thy faith hath saved thee." Luke xviii. 42. Manifestly the power to restore sight was not in the man's faith. The power was in Christ, but faith was the channel of its conveyance from Christ to the blind man. So in the matter of salvation. There is in Christ exhaustless saving power, but that this power may become available to salvation, there must be faith in Christ. Then the believer's faith saves him instrumentally, while Christ saves him effectually and meritoriously. See Rom. x. 4; 1 Cor. i. 30. It is the province of faith to receive Christ and trust in him for salvation. I mean that the believer receives Christ as he is offered in the gospel, receives him fully, wholly, heartily, gladly, cheerfully. Never forget that faith has respect to Christ as the Saviour.

REMARKS.

I. We see from this text the first two things to preach.

II. We can detect spurious repentance.

III. We see what genuine, saving faith is.

IV. Have you repented of your sins and believed in Christ?

ONE LORD, ONE FAITH, ONE BAPTISM.

One Lord, one faith, one baptism.—Eph. iv. 5.

In the third verse of this chapter there is mention of the unity of the Spirit, and there are seven truths named in the text and context, each of which is an unexpanded argument in favor of unity. To every one of these truths the numeral epithet *one* is applied. There is one body. How strong the argument furnished by this fact as a reason for Christian unity! So of the one Spirit, the one hope, the one God and Father of all. But it is my purpose to call attention to the one Lord, one faith, one baptism. My subject will be identical with the text. Let us contemplate the three unities in their order.

I. *One Lord.* The reference is to the Lord Jesus Christ. The Spirit is named in the verse preceding, and the Father in the verse succeeding, the text. We are thus taught the doctrine of the Trinity. The second person of the sacred Three is Lord. The term means Sovereign, Master, Prince, Ruler.

1. *Jesus is Lord in this sense.* This is a mediatorial title. It is given to Christ because of his official position. In consequence of his work of mediation he has been invested with universal dominion. The angel that announced his birth to the shepherds, said: "To you is born this day a Saviour, who is Christ the Lord." Luke ii. 11. Peter said on Pentecost: "God hath made that same Jesus whom ye have crucified, both Lord and Christ." Acts ii. 36. In Philippians ii. 5–11, the universal lordship of Jesus is clearly taught. The administration of the Divine Government is in his hands, as we learn from the second Psalm. As Lord, he must reign till he puts all enemies under his feet. The last act which he, as Lord Mediator is to perform, will be the judging of the world. Then he will deliver up the mediatorial kingdom, as we are taught in 1 Cor. xv. 24–28.

2. *Jesus is the object of faith because he is Lord.* We have seen that because he humbled himself he was exalted to universal lordship. The death of the cross makes him the Author of salvation, and therefore, the object of faith. Salvation was impossible without his death. His was an atoning death, meeting the demands of the law. He is, therefore, the end of the law for righteousness. The law is magnified by his obedience and blood. He is supremely suitable as the object of faith. He is the God-man, and therefore the merits of his death are infinite. As the God-man he comes between God and man, and acts as Mediator. God is well pleased with his righteousness; and the sinner, to be saved, must also be well pleased. His approval must be expressed by believing on the Lord Jesus. This brings me to my second point.

II. *One faith.* The one faith embraces the one Lord Faith in Christ is substantially one. It may be weak or strong; it may be exercised by persons of every nation, and in every variety of circumstances; but it is in essence one. It is a personal act terminating on a personal object. The belief of a proposition, or any series of propositions, cannot save. For example, a belief that Jesus is the Christ does not save. This is the belief of a proposition. There must be trust in Christ as a person. We read of believing *in* or *on* Christ. In the Greek it is usually *into* Christ, as if the roots of faith penetrate into his person and mediatorial character to find nourishment. In Acts xvi. 31, we read, "Believe on the Lord Jesus Christ." Here the idea seems to be that of resting all the weighty interests of salvation on Christ, even as a superstructure rests its weight on its foundation. Faith receives Christ. John i. 12. It receives the one Lord. It unites to him, and from the union results the imputation of his righteousness with all that salvation implies. The saving merit which is in Christ is appropriated by the believer.

Faith effects in a sinner's state the wonderful transition from condemnation to justification. Faith cleaves to the Lord Jesus—the one faith to the one Lord.

III. *One baptism.* This text is in perfect accord with the Commission of Christ, as recorded in Matt. xxviii. 19, 20; Mark xvi. 15, 16. The gospel, which tells of Christ, is to be preached to all. He that believes is to be baptized. When the one Lord is received by the one faith, baptism is to be administered. The one baptism is as specific as the one faith or the one Lord. It is the baptism of a believer, for it is a profession of faith. Unbelievers, or those incapable of faith, have nothing to do with this baptism. The act of baptism is immersion. This is the meaning of the word. For this reason it is symbolic of a burial. Rom. vi. 4; Col. ii. 12. For this reason it represents the believer's death to sin and resurrection to newness of life. Knowing baptism to be immersion, we understand what is said about going down into, and coming up out of the water. Acts viii. 38, 39. To constitute the one baptism, there must be a believer in the one Lord and the specific act, expressed by the word "baptism," a word that denotes, in its common, ordinary, literal meaning an *immersion.* To have one baptism, there cannot be more than one class of subjects, nor more than one act. Think of this. Two classes of subjects and two acts must make two baptisms, but the text says one baptism. There is only one.

REMARKS.

I. There is but one Lord and Saviour.

II. Do you believe in him, and have you professed your faith in baptism?

III. How important is the gospel order! If we transpose or invert the terms Lord, faith, baptism, the beauty and also the import of the divine arrangement at once disappear.

WHAT A CHURCH IS.

But if I tarry long, that thou mayest know how thou oughtest to behave thyself in the house of God, which is the church of the living God, the pillar and ground of the truth.—1 Tim. iii. 15.

Paul about to visit Macedonia, requested Timothy to remain at Ephesus. It was well that the apostle was separated from his "son in the faith"; for the separation occasioned the writing of this Epistle, which is full of precious truth and important instruction. Among other things, Paul refers specially to the character and qualifications of bishops and deacons. Then he adds the words of the text. In giving the result of my reflections on this text I will dwell on this subject:

WHAT A CHURCH IS.

I inquire as to—

I. *The literal meaning of the term.* The word translated church in the New Testament is, in three places, rendered "assembly." See Acts xix. 32, 39, 41. Assembly is a good translation; and in its Scriptural sense, a church of Christ is either a local congregation of saints, or it is the aggregate of the redeemed. It is employed in the latter sense, as I think, in Eph. v. 25–27. In a very large majority of cases it dedenotes a local congregation. According to the New Testament those embodied in a church are *called out*—out from the world and sin. Baptism draws a line of distinction between a church and the world. A church then is a congregation of Christ's baptized disciples, united in the belief of what he has said, and covenanting to do what he has commanded. It will be seen, in view of this definition, that the pre-requisites of church membership are both moral and ritual. The moral are repentance and faith; the ritual qualification is baptism. So much for the literal meaning of the word church.

II. *The figurative meaning of the term.* I shall not attempt to give an exhaustive view of this meaning, but confine myself to the two forms of expression in the text:

1. *House of God.* A church is by figure of speech called *a* house of God. The text says *the*, but the article is not in the Greek; nor is there an article before any noun in the text except the one translated *truth*, very properly *the truth.* The imagery employed may have been suggested by the Temple of Diana in Ephesus, one of the "seven wonders of the world." If so, we see the force of the words "living God," a living God—there is no article in the original—in contradistinction from a *lifeless* idol. Diana was an imaginary being; our God is a *real* being, and the source of being to all creatures. But it may be that the Temple at Jerusalem suggested the form of expression. That was God's house. He was said to dwell there. The Temple as his dwelling-place was a type of a Christian heart and a Christian church. 1 Cor. iii. 16, 17; 2 Cor. vi. 16. We see the beauty of this arrangement. The individual heart is by regeneration fitted for God's dwelling-place. Then a company of regenerate persons coming together as a church, the church is God's dwelling-place, because the renewed hearts of those forming it were previously places in which he dwelt. If a church, so-called, is not composed of regenerate persons, God does not dwell there, even as he does not dwell in unregenerate hearts. "House of God!" What an idea! Refer to what Solomon said at the dedication of the Temple. 1 Kings viii. 27. What said Jesus? John xiv. 23. It is infinite honor for God to dwell in an individual heart, or in a church. Often contemplate a church as God's house, his dwelling-place.

2. *Pillar and ground of the truth.* These are controverted words. Some say they mean that a church rests on the truth, and others say that a church maintains, upholds, and instrumentally preserves the truth. I see no objection to the union of the two views. A church rests on Christ, and as he is the

truth, in this sense it rests on the truth. I doubt not the other view is the prominent one in the text. I think the terms "pillar" and "ground" convey the idea of support. It is the responsible province of a church to maintain the truth—the truth

a. Concerning God.
b. Concerning man.
c. Concerning salvation through Christ.
d. Concerning regeneration by the Holy Spirit.
e. Concerning justification by faith.
f. Concerning the ordinances of the gospel.
g. Concerning good works.
h. Concerning the resurrection and the eternal state.

The more truth a church holds in the love of it, the better and purer it is. This suggests the propriety of church discipline in the cases of those who depart from the truth in *doctrine* or *practice.*

III. *How church members should conduct themselves.* "That thou mayest know how thou oughtest to behave thyself in the house of God." There is an obligation resting on every member. "How thou oughtest to behave thyself," that is, conduct thyself. The dignity and comfort of a family depend very much on the manner in which its members act. The phrase "house of God" is strongly suggestive of holiness. God is holy, and a church, his dwelling-place, should be holy. David said of the literal temple, "Holiness becometh thine house, O Lord, forever." This may be said of every church, considered as God's house. Holiness invites, and sin repels the divine presence. The officers of a church should conduct themselves with propriety. The pastor of a church has his duties. He is to feed the flock with spiritual food. Deacons have their duties. It is their business to attend specially to the financial interests of the church. There are duties com mon to all church members. All should—

a. *Maintain fellowship with God.*
b. *Regulate their words and acts according to the gospel.*
c. *Love one another, and show their love in suitable ways.*
d. *Not forsaking the assembling of themselves together.*
e. *Labor for the conversion and salvation of sinners.*

This last is probably the most imperative obligation resting on a church, namely, to hold forth as a light the word of life, that those in darkness may see it and be led to turn to God.

If the foregoing exposition is correct, the text may be translated thus: "But if I tarry long, that thou mayest know how thou oughtest to conduct thyself in a house of God, which is a church of a living God, a pillar and a ground of the truth."

AN UNFAITHFUL CHURCH IN DANGER OF EXTINCTION.

. . . I will come unto thee quickly, and will remove thy candlestick out of his place, except thou repent.—Rev. ii. 5.

This is solemn language, for it intimates that an unfaithful church may become extinct. Who, acquainted with ecclesiastical history, can deny this? How many churches once flourishing, have no existence now! How many moral lights, once shining brightly, have been eclipsed, shrouded in total darkness! This has been the penalty for disobedience. The church, in what I may call the generic sense of the term, will never become extinct. The gates of hell will not prevail against her. But local churches may lose their visibility. Where is now the church of Ephesus? It is no more. The candlestick has been removed. The theme naturally suggested by the text is this:

AN UNFAITHFUL CHURCH IN DANGER OF EXTINCTION.

In illustration of this theme I will consider—

I. *The purposes of church organization.* What are they?

1. *The spiritual improvement of Christians.* The Saviour recognized and sanctified the social principle in the establishment of churches. His disciples are brought together, embodied by means of their church relations. A church is compared by Paul to a human body, and all the members are to have a sympathetic concern for one another. This concern must have its origin in mutual love. But how are church members to promote mutual spiritual improvement? I answer:

a. By frequently meeting together and maintaining the worship of God. Heb. x. 25.

b. By hearkening to the teachings of the pastor, whose business it is to feed the sheep and the lambs. John xxi. 15, 16, 17; Acts xx. 28; 1 Peter v. 2.

c. By exhorting one another and praying for one another Heb. iii. 13; James v. 16.

d. By stimulating to love and good works. Heb. x. 24.

e. By admonishing those who sin. Matt. xviii. 15; Luke xvii. 3.

f. By withdrawing fellowship from the disorderly. Matt. xviii. 17; 2 Thess. iii. 6.

The question in 1 Cor. v. 6, must not be forgotten. These things, if done by church members, will promote spiritual improvement.

2. *The salvation of sinners.* Every church must look to this. Every member must strive for the conversion of souls. The light of a church must shine. Matt. v. 16; Phil. 2. 15; 1 Peter ii. 12. It is the business of a church to sustain the ministry of the word, not only with reference to the edification of its members, but with a view to the conversion of sinners. Individual effort must enforce the appeals of the pulpit. Personal labor cannot be dispensed with. A church that does nothing for the cause of missions cannot be in a healthful state. She has the bread of heaven in her custody, and must distribute it to earth's starving millions.

3. *The promotion of the divine glory.* This is a purpose superior to every other. It is the supreme purpose of church organization, and is accomplished by means of the two purposes just referred to. That is to say, when saints are edified and sinners saved, God is glorified; when they are not, God is dishonored. This is too plain to be called in question.

II. *A church that fails to execute the purposes of its organization is in danger of becoming extinct.* Why is this the case?

1. *Because such a church is peculiarly liable to embrace false doctrines.* The moral state of individuals and churches has much to do in the espousal or rejection of correct sentiments. The propagators of error make an easy prey of a lifeless, lethargic church. When a church rejects fundamental doctrines or nullifies the ordinances of the gospel, it forfeits the right to be called a church, and becomes "a synagogue of Satan."

2. *Because such a church must decline in numbers.* We have seen that the salvation of sinners is one object contemplated in church organization. Now if a church is not instrumental in saving sinners, how is its number to be increased? There will be a decrease of numbers. Death is ever at work. Church members die as well as others. If no additions are made to a church it must, in the lapse of years cease to be. All can see how this is.

3. *Because such a church giving a false representation of Christianity, God, jealous of his honor, may remove the candlestick out of its place.* Such a church gives a slanderous report of the religion of Christ. God may see that it is better for the interests of his cause that so unfaithful a church should not be. He may see that one enemy in the camp of the saints can do more injury than a thousand foes without. He may take to heaven some of the spiritual members of such a church, if there are spiritual members, and others

under his guiding providence may seek new homes, and the worldly-minded may go back to the world. Then the extinction is complete. The candlestick is removed. Darkness takes the place of light. Sad, sad change!

III. *Though a church may be in danger of extinction, repentance will prevent so deplorable a doom.* "Except thou repent." Without repentance the candlestick is to be removed. Nothing else will prevent its removal. There must be deep contrition on account of the failure to carry out the purposes of church organization. Tears, lamentations, confessions, and prayers, are imperatively called for. There must be amendment. Reformation will show the sincerity of repentance, and nothing else will. Repentance, followed by reformation, will secure the permanence of the candlestick in its place.

REMARKS.

I. Is the church of which you are a member like that of Ephesus?

II. If so, let the work of repentance begin at once.

III. How good is God to forgive repenting backsliders!

SPIRITUAL PROTECTION AND REFRESHMENT.

And a man shall be as an hiding-place from the wind, and a covert from the tempest; as rivers of waters in a dry place, as the shadow of a great rock in a weary land.—Isa. xxxii. 2.

Some have supposed that Hezekiah is the king referred to in the preceding verse. If so, he must have been only a type of Christ; for in reading the text, we involuntarily exclaim: Behold a greater than Hezekiah is here. True, our attention is directed to "a man," but we know of "the man Christ Jesus," who is Mediator between God and men. I take it for granted that he is the hiding-place. I deduce from the text this theme:

SPIRITUAL PROTECTION AND REFRESHMENT.

Fix your thoughts on—

I. *Spiritual protection.* This is indicated by two expressions which claim our attention:

1. *A hiding-place from the wind.* Evidently the term wind does not refer to a gentle breeze, but to a violent gale, to a storm so furious as to make protection a vital necessity. We can easily imagine such a storm raging with desolating violence. How great the danger, and how important to have a hiding-place! This is true literally. It is also true spiritually. There is the storm of God's wrath against sin. I know that there is a liberal theology, falsely so-called, which denies that there is wrath in God. This view is in direct conflict with such Scriptures as the following: John iii. 36, Rom. i. 18; Eph. v. 6. This wrath is not some abstract thing, but personal indignation in view of sin; and, as sin cannot exist apart from sinners, it is indignation against sinners. God's wrath grows out of the purity of his nature. All good and holy beings feel indignation against sin in proportion to their goodness and holiness. What then shall I say of the intensity of God's indignation against sin? It is to be measured by the holiness of his nature. There is wrath in God, and because of this fact he is the more worthy of adoration. How can this wrath be appeased? By the removal of the cause that excites it. That cause, as we have seen, is sin. Here then we see how "the man Christ Jesus" becomes a hiding-place. See John i. 29; Heb. ix. 26; and also 1 Thess. i. 10. Jesus delivers from the wrath to come. How? By the atoning provision made by his death for the pardon of sin, and the consequent remission of the penalty of the law of which sin is the transgression. Thus he becomes a hiding-place for the poor sinner exposed to the wrath of God. Here you can see the meaning of his words

in Matt. xi. 28. We see, too, the import of Rom. v. 1. There is peace with God through Christ, because Christ is the hiding-place of the sinner who flees from the storm of God's wrath. There is protection in the cross.

2. *A covert from the tempest.* This is the second of the two forms of expression I have referred to as suggesting the idea of spiritual protection. It means in substance what the other expression means. I need not therefore enlarge on it, but leave it to your reflection. When the tempest is on its march of desolation, how imperatively is a covert needed! What a covert do we find in Christ! A sure protection from all danger and all evil. Rom. viii. 33, 34. Protection in Christ. We may now see why Paul wished to "be found in him." He desired ample and certain protection.

II. *Spiritual refreshment.* This also is indicated by two forms of expression:

1. *Rivers of water in a dry place.* We may have known by experience something of the discomforts of literal drought, and we have heard a great deal more than we have known. Imagine a sandy desert, on which the sun pours his burning rays. The traveler is parched with thirst, almost ready to faint and die from exhaustion, and desiring water more than all earthly blessings. As he drags his weary feet along he lifts up his eyes and sees a river of water, sees it in the midst of the dry places about him. How soon he slakes his thirst, is satisfied and refreshed! So "the man, Christ Jesus," who is a hiding-place, is "as rivers of water in a dry place." There is spiritual refreshment. As literal water satisfies literal thirst, so the spiritual water that Christ gives, the symbol of his grace, satisfies the thirst of the soul. The two kinds of water are contrasted. John iv. 13, 14. He that drinks of the water that Christ gives is refreshed in his spirit. Protection is outward, refreshment is inward. Justification is something done *for* us; regeneration is something done *in*

us, that gives us a taste for spiritual things, and causes us to enjoy them. Hence there is spiritual refreshment. There is what Paul calls the peace of God. There is abundance of joy. Christ is "as rivers of water in a dry place." All this earth is a dry place. We are dependent on Christ for rivers of water.

2. *The shadow of a great rock in a weary land.* By a figure of speech the land is said to be weary, instead of the traveler who, under the pressure of scorching heat, comes to a great rock that casts its grateful shadow. Availing himself of the cool shade, he is refreshed. So there is spiritual refreshment in Christ. We have in him a thousand times more than is symbolized by the shadow of a great rock in a weary land. The soul feasts on his love. Jesus says, "These things have I spoken unto you—that your joy might be full."

QUERIES:

I. Is Christ spiritual protection to you?
II. Do you find spiritual refreshment in him?

TRUST IN GOD PRODUCTIVE OF PEACE.

Thou wilt keep him in perfect peace, whose mind is stayed on thee: because he trusteth in thee.—Isa. xxvi. 3.

The Bible says much about trust in God. It requires us to trust in him, and assures us that it is better to trust in the Lord than to put confidence in men, even in princes. It declares that those who trust in the Lord shall be as Mount Zion, which cannot be removed, but abideth forever. There are many happy consequences resulting from this trust. In the text our attention is directed to one of these consequences, namely, peace. The matter for us to consider, is—

TRUST IN GOD PRODUCTIVE OF PEACE.

The tendency of this trust to inspire peace may be seen in such considerations as the following:

I. *God is Almighty.* David says: "God has spoken once; twice have I heard this; that power belongeth unto God." Contemplate this power as exerted in the creation of all things, and as exercised in the preservation of all things. The telescope reveals numberless worlds to the astronomer. It was almighty power that brought those worlds into existence and keeps them in the places assigned them. All manifestations of power, as seen in the movements of matter, are traceable to God. The power of finite spirits is secondary, and is derived from the Supreme Spirit. In the highest sense all power is God's. This fact brings peace to those who trust in him; for they know that in his sovereign pleasure he will exert his power in their behalf.

2. *God is everywhere.* The ancient heathen had local gods, and the power of these gods was, according to the teachings of mythology, restricted in its operation to their respective spheres of action. How great would be the disadvantages of trusting in a God confined to localities, if there could be such a God! Jehovah is omnipresent. We cannot go out of his dominions or beyond his jurisdiction. He is ever present with his creatures, all his creatures, and graciously present with all who trust in him. The greatness of his power could not of itself create peace if he were not everywhere present to exert his power. Psalm cxxxix. 7–12.

3. *God knows all things.* We are not able to appreciate adequately the divine omniscience; for our faculties are quite limited. We know but little. The past, the present, and the future, are all known to God, and he therefore knows just what we need. Nothing can occur that will take him by surprise. No exigencies, no contingencies, can arise, for

which he is unprepared. How precious the peace derived from trusting in a God who knows all things, and whose knowledge directs the exercise of his power, in all places!

4. *God is good.* His power, omnipresence, and omniscience, apart from his goodness, would not bring to the soul the "perfect peace" to which the text refers. His goodness disposes him to employ his power for the benefit of those who put their trust in him. It prompts him to make his omnipresence and omniscience practically beneficial to them. "The Lord is good, a strong hold in the day of trouble; and he knoweth them that trust in him." Nahum i. 7. Jehovah is the fountain of goodness, and his goodness is inseparable from his glory. Hence, when Moses prayed, "Show me thy glory," the Lord said, "I will make all my goodness pass before thee." Ex. xxxiii. 18, 19. There is peace to those who trust in the Lord, because he is good. They see how his goodness can be exercised through Jesus Christ. They see that the plan of redemption which the gospel reveals meets all the necessities of their condition as helpless sinners, and "being justified by faith, they have peace with God." Rom. v. 1. The peace of God keeps [*garrisons*] their hearts and minds through Christ Jesus. Phil. iv. 7. They have the peace which the Saviour bequeathed to his disciples in the memorable words, "Peace I leave with you, my peace I give unto you: not as the world giveth, give I unto you. Let not your heart be troubled, neither let it be afraid." John xiv. 27.

5. *God makes all things work together for good to those who trust in him.* He who does this has all things under his control. There is no world in which he does not act. There is no event, great or small, over which he does not preside. All things are either the effects of his active agency or the results of his providential permission. Nothing occurs which he does not permit. Commotions, revolutions, and wars, with

all their bloody accompaniments, take place because he suffers them to take place. Still the wrath of man praises him. He brings good out of evil, joy out of sorrow, and light out of darkness. He makes all the trials and sufferings of his people promotive of their spiritual welfare. When he chastens them, it is for their profit, that they may be partakers of his holiness. Heb. xii. 10. In all this he is executing his infinitely wise plans for the glory of his name and the good of those who put their trust in him. In view of the considerations now presented, it is easy to see that trust in God is productive of peace.

REMARKS.

I. Is this peace yours?

II. If not, it is because you do not trust in the Lord.

III. There is no peace to the wicked.

PRESENT CONFIDENCE INSPIRED BY PAST EXPERIENCE.

The Lord that delivered me out of the paw of the lion, and out of the paw of the bear, he will deliver me out of the hand of this Philistine.—1 Sam. xvii. 37.

The Israelites were involved in war with the Philistines. It was a time of great anxiety. King Saul and his army were fearful as to the issue of the contest, while the masses of the people were dismayed. The general feeling of fear was increased by the haughty bearing of Goliath, the giant of Gath. He for forty days defied the hosts of Israel, proposing that a contest between himself and any Israelite should be decisive, and therefore final. David now appears on the scene, and accepts the challenge of the giant. Saul tries to dissuade him from so rash a step (verse 33); David replies, (verses 34–36). Then he spoke the words of the text, which is suggestive of this theme:

PRESENT CONFIDENCE INSPIRED BY PAST EXPERIENCE.

We will consider—

I. *Past experience.* The experience to which David refers was very impressive, and he could not forget it. He was a shepherd, and his devotion to his father's flock was beautiful. So strong was his attachment to the sheep and the lambs that when one of the latter was taken out of the flock by a lion, he rescued it and killed the lion. So of a bear on another occasion; for two occasions are referred to. "Thy servant slew," verse 36. It was no exertion of ordinary human power that enabled him to do this. Notice, he ascribes these exploits to the Lord. He obtained help from Jehovah. He had a conscious experience that the Lord was with him and delivered him from peril. David had no doubt often received help from on high, but he names only these two prominent instances. So much for David's past experience. What about your past experience? It has not been like David's in one respect, but in another it has been the same. That is to say, the Lord has delivered you as he delivered David. Go back in thought to the period of your conviction of sin. I mean the time when you were convinced that you were a sinner in perishing need of a Saviour. You made the jailer's question yours. Acts xvi. 30. You felt that God was in the right and you in the wrong. You felt guilty before him, and justly condemned by his law. Your prayer was that of the publican, "God be merciful to me, a sinner." Was he not merciful? You hearkened to the words of Jesus, "Come unto me, . . . and I will give you rest." Did you not find "rest"? Did you not learn the truth of Rom. v. 1? Did you not have a precious experience of the saving grace of God? Did he not bring you up "out of an horrible pit, out of the miry clay"? This is David's language on another occasion. Did not God take you into fellowship with himself, lavishing on you all the sacred pleasures of reconciliation? Did he not adopt and own you as his child? Did you not enjoy the spirit of adoption? With some of you many days have passed since then. You have experienced temptations, trials, afflictions, bereavements, and, it may be, persecutions. Can you not say to-day, "Ebenezer"? Have you not found the grace of God sufficient for you? Has his arm ever failed of its strength? Has not the Lord delivered you as surely as he did David? Have you not experienced his delivering mercy in every time of need?

II. *Present confidence.* In David's case this was inspired by past experience. He said: "The Lord will deliver me out of the hand of this Philistine." Why did he have this confidence? Because the Lord had delivered him "out of the paw of the lion, and out of the paw of the bear." This was the basis of his confidence. He reasoned from what the Lord had done to what he would do. Can you not reason in the same way? Must you not? Ought you not? Is it not both your duty and privilege? You should have present confidence in the Lord on account of what he has done for you in times past. You profess to be a Christian. Who has made you a Christian? God This is clear from John i. 13. Why did he make you a Christian? You had no claim on him. There was nothing in you to excite in the divine mind any other feeling than that of pity. It was therefore his purpose of grace that led him to make the great change in you by which you became a Christian. There was no merit in you, but demerit. It required omnipotent grace to triumph over the demerit; but it did triumph, and therefore you are a child of God. Is there at present, or will there be in future, an occasion for a display of greater grace than was exercised in your regeneration? I suppose not. Is there not ground then for present confidence, that God will do what you need to-day, to-morrow, and through the pilgrimage of life? See how Paul reasons in Rom. v. 10: viii. 32. Here we go back to the past. God laid, in the death of his Son, the basis of our reconciliation with him when we were his enemies. "Much more" shall he help and bless us "being reconciled." If God "spared not his own Son, but delivered him up for us all, how shall he not with him also freely give us all things?' Our past knowledge and experience of what God has done, may well be the inspiration of present confidence. His immutability makes it certain that he will now, and in time to come, act toward his people as he did in making them his people. That is, he will manifest his grace. What he has done is the best guarantee of what he will do. You say you are very unworthy. Yes, but God knew how unworthy you were and would be when he called you by his grace. If your unworthiness is now to be a barrier to the reception of the grace you need, it would have been a barrier to the reception of the grace that made you a Christian. You need God's help to-day. Have confidence in him and expect it in view of the past. You must die ere long. Believe that God will be with you then because he has been with you. In short, let past experience inspire present confidence.

REMARKS.

I. Think often of what the Lord has done for you.

II. Trust him for all you need now and forever.

PLEASING GOD.

Not as pleasing men, but God, which trieth our hearts.—1 Thess. ii. 4.

Paul is here giving an account of his first visit to Thessalonica. He had been shamefully persecuted at Philippi, but instead of giving up his ministerial work he became more earnest in its performance. He tells the Thessalonians that he spoke to them "the gospel of God with much contention," that his "exhortation was not of deceit," that having been entrusted with the gospel, he preached it not with a view to please men, but God. This was the object at which he aimed, and this should be our object. Your attention is therefore called to the subject of—

PLEASING GOD.

For the purpose of elucidating this subject I may say—

I. *God deserves to be pleased.* This appears at once in view of the fact that he is the Almighty Creator. It has been his pleasure to create what we call matter. He has made use of this matter in the formation of planets and suns and worlds. He has arranged it according to his will. But this matter, whatever its movements may be, has no intention of pleasing God. It has no intelligence, and therefore no purpose. I refer specially to rational beings when I say that God deserves to be pleased. Refer to Rev. iv. 11. Notice specially the words, "for thy pleasure they are and were created." The motive prompting creation was in the Creator. It was optional with God to create or not. He chose to create, and to do so for his pleasure. That he deserves to be pleased, is a truth as clear as the light of day. If so, his creatures are under obligation to please him. This is true of every angel, every man, every demon. There can be no obligation to God unless there is obligation to please him, for this is inseparable from the obligation to love him. God deserves to be pleased, for he is pleased with that only which is right. So far then as his creatures please him they do right.

II. *How God is pleased.* All his creatures may please him by loving him. You can conceive of no rational being with whose love God would not be pleased. The love would be a recognition of his worthiness of love.

But there are ways of pleasing God which have special reference to men, and to men as sinners. How then do human beings please God?

1. *By hearty repentance.* This is a duty incumbent on sinners only. Repentance is such a change of mind in regard to sin as involves sorrow for it, also hatred of it, and a purpose to forsake it. Sin is the transgression of God's law, and the law is a transcript of his moral character. As God loves his law he must be displeased when it is violated. If so, he is pleased when sorrow is felt for its violation; for the sorrow recognizes the goodness of the law and of the lawgiver.

2. *By a cordial acceptance of Christ.* When Jesus was baptized the voice of God the Father was heard, saying, "This is my beloved Son, in whom I am well pleased." If God is well pleased with his Son, he would have us well pleased with him also. We cannot better please God than by being pleased with his Son, the proof of which is to be seen in our reception of him as the Saviour. God in sending his Son into the world could not be indifferent as to the object of his mission. That object was the salvation of sinners; but it cannot be accomplished unless Christ is accepted as the Saviour. God must therefore be pleased with those who thankfully receive Christ, and displeased with those who reject him.

3. *By showing ourselves his friends before men.* The piety of the heart is of the greatest importance, but it is not of itself sufficient. There must be consecration of life to the service of God. A baptismal profession of faith must be followed by conduct in accordance with such profession. Phil. i. 27. While we are to make no parade of our religion, we must ever be willing and even glad to be known as the Lord's servants.

4. *By cheerful resignation to his will.* God's will is always right, and when it is his will to afflict us we must not murmur, but say, "The will of the Lord be done." We must say this when the dying hour comes. God will ever be pleased when we will as he wills.

III. *A consciousness that we please God is a source of high satisfaction.* This is evident because—

I. *He is perfect in judgment.* There is no appeal from his decision. He tries the heart and tests the purity of the motives. Blessed are those on whom the smile of his approval rests. If the God of heaven is pleased with us, we may well have exultant satisfaction.

2. *This consciousness is a shield from the reproaches of men.* When our acts are misconstrued, our words misinterpreted, and our motives misconceived, how delightful to know that, whatever men may think or say, God is pleased with us! The high satisfaction arising from this consciousness is worth more than "gold; yea, than much fine gold."

3. *It brightens the prospect of going into the presence of God.* Think of it—going to Him who is pleased with you, and who will evermore imparadise you in his smiles!

REMARKS.

I. We have in this subject the true principle of action. An archangel knows no higher aspiration than a desire to please God.

II. Is God pleased with you? with the state of your heart and the manner of your life?

III. Some of you have never done anything with a view to please God. How wicked your hearts must be!

LIKENESS TO CHRIST.

Let this mind be in you, which was also in Christ Jesus.—Phil. ii. 5.

We are told that Christ left us an example that we "should follow his steps," and that we are under obligation to "walk even as he walked"; that is, to live as he lived. This walking or living refers chiefly to conduct, behavior; but in the text our attention is directed to that state of mind in Christ, which was the inspiration of his conduct. He acted as he did because he thought as he did, and felt as he did. We are required to be like him. This is the doctrine of the text:

LIKENESS TO CHRIST.

Let us consider—

I. *In what respects we should be like Christ.* I present the following particulars:

1. *In his zeal for the divine glory.* There was in Christ nothing more manifest than this zeal. The sacred flame burnt with unceasing constancy on the altar of his heart. We see in John ii. 14–18, what occurred at the beginning of his ministry. We may refer also to what he said in John iv 34, but specially to his words, "Father, glorify thy name." John xii. 28. When he urged this petition, the agony of the garden and the death of the cross were at hand. Dismissing from his mind his personal sufferings, he said, "Father, glorify thy name." The glory of God was the object nearest and dearest to his heart. To be like Christ we must have his zeal for the divine glory. This point of resemblance to him is indispensable.

2. *In his self-sacrificing love for men.* This was in perfect accord with his zeal. His great purpose was that God should be glorified in man's salvation. To accomplish this object something must be done for men. That something proceeded from his love and could have no other origin. Oh, what love! Think what it prompted him to become, to do, to suffer. You see at every step the self-sacrificing quality of that love. Jesus loved men in their complete persons, body and soul. We must love them too. We may not be required to die for them, as Jesus did; but to be like him we must, in our measure, love them as he did.

3. *In his humility.* He was meek and lowly in heart. We see his humility in the different steps of his condescension,

beginning with laying aside his glory and reaching the lowest point in the grave. If we would be like Christ, pride must be expelled from our hearts. There is nothing in us to be proud of, but everything to inspire lowliness of mind. It requires humility to make us like Christ. This was the mind which was in him.

4. *In returning good for evil.* It has been said that to return evil for evil is man-like, to return evil for good is devil-like, and to return good for evil is God-like. Jesus did the last. How kindly he taught his enemies! How earnestly he prayed for those nailing him to the cross! We are not like Christ unless we have the disposition to return good for evil, blessing for cursing. Stephen imbibed the spirit of Jesus, as we may see from Acts vii. 60.

5. *In his resignation to the will of God.* He says: "For I came down from heaven, not to do mine own will, but the will of him that sent me." John vi. 38. In Heb. x. 5–7, we see the conformity of his will to the will of God. In his agony in Gethsemane he prayed, "Father, if thou be willing, remove this cup from me: nevertheless, not my will. but thine be done." Luke xxii. 42. This was perfect resignation. Let this mind be in you. We must be like Christ in his feelings of conformity and resignation to the will of God. We must be resigned to God's will, not merely because we cannot help ourselves, but because we believe that his will is right and ought to be done.

II. *How to acquire likeness to Christ.* I name the following things:

1. *Make his character a constant study.* Occasional and superficial study will not suffice. Analyze the excellences of his character. Consider them in their isolated glory and beauty. Then combine them and contemplate their united perfection and splendor. Such a study of any merely human character would discover defects: but not so in the character

of Christ. It will bear the closest investigation. The more microscopic the examination, the more glorious will it appear. Study the character of Christ by day and by night, if you would be like him.

2. *Let his word dwell in you richly.* This is a divine command. Col. iii. 16. It must be obeyed in connection with a study of his character. *Dwell,* not enter and depart, but *abide,* not scantily, but richly, its influence diffusing itself through all the powers of the soul. This word of Christ teaches us to love what Christ loves, and to hate what Christ hates. It teaches us his will. It is the means of sanctification, which is likeness to him.

3. *There must be much prayer for the Holy Spirit.* The Spirit is the Glorifier of Christ. He glorifies him by making his disciples like unto him, who is the Supreme Model of perfection. The Spirit is given, and *how,* we learn from Luke xi. 13. Languid, lukewarm prayer, will not do; earnest, importunate supplication is required.

REMARKS.

I. How desirable is likeness to Christ!

II. We may well mourn that we are not more like him.

III. Likeness to him is not an accident, but the result of earnest striving.

LOOKING TO JESUS.

Looking unto Jesus.—Heb. xii. 2.

What a glorious object invites our contemplations! It is our privilege to behold the Lamb of God. Ponder the theme:

LOOKING TO JESUS.

These words imply faith in Christ, and the direction of the attention to him. As he is enthroned in heaven far beyond the limits of mortal vision, we can only look to him by faith —with the eye of the mind.

I. *In what respects are we to look to Jesus?* I answer:

1. *In his blameless life, as furnishing an example for us to copy.*

2. *In his atoning death, as the basis of our salvation.*

3. *As our interceding Advocate in heaven.*

II. *Benefits of looking to Jesus.* I name only a few:

1. *The improvement of the Christian graces.*

2. *The love of the world is crucified.*

3. *Holiness of life is promoted.*

4. *The fear of death is subdued.*

REMARKS.

I. It is a great privilege to look to Jesus.

II. There is danger of looking away from him.

III. Looking to Jesus anticipates the employment of heaven.

IV. Let sinners look to Jesus as the Saviour, before they see him as their final Judge.

HOLDING FORTH THE WORD OF LIFE.

Holding forth the word of life.—Phil. ii. 16.

The gospel is called the word of God, the word of Christ, the word of his grace, the word of truth, the word of faith, and the word of salvation. In the text it is termed the word of life, and Christians are required to hold it forth. As the text and the theme it furnishes are coincident, we fix our thoughts on—

HOLDING FORTH THE WORD OF LIFE.

It will be our business to—

I. *Contemplate the gospel as the word of life.* It is properly thus designated because—

1. *It makes known the way of life.* I employ the term life as denoting both spiritual and eternal life. By nature we are dead in sin; for sin has extinguished the principle of spiritual life which man enjoyed in his unfallen state. The gospel alone tells us how this principle may be re-obtained. Nature and reason and human philosophy cannot tell. Regenerating grace is a gospel idea, exclusively so. The gospel, too, directs our attention to eternal life. 2 Tim. i. 10. We are obviously dependent on the Bible for any satisfactory conception of futurity. The old heathen philosophers had some confused views of the soul's immortality; but of the resurrection and future life of the body they had no thought. In the Old Testament we have the doctrine of immortality in a state of comparative obscurity; the gospel brings it out of obscurity into the light of open day. The resurrection of Jesus confirms all the gospel says.

2. *It is the means of imparting spiritual life to the dead in sin.* Some think it detracts from the glory of God to say that he regenerates the soul by means of the gospel. God employs means in the natural world.

> What is his creation less
> Than a capacious reservoir of means
> Formed for his use, and ready at his will?—*Cowper.*

Why may not God also use means in the moral world? The teaching of the Scriptures is plain as to the instrumentality of divine truth in regeneration. 1 Cor. iv. 15; James i. 18; 1 Peter i. 23. The Holy Spirit, in effecting the great change, makes use of truth previously lodged in the understanding. Thus the gospel which makes known the way of life is the means of imparting life.

3. *It is the instrument of guidance to eternal life.* Our Heavenly Leader makes it the means by which he conducts spiritual pilgrims through the wilderness of this world to the land of promise. "Thou shalt guide me with thy counsel,

and afterward receive me to glory." Psalm lxxiii. 24. The same gospel which makes known the way of life, and instrumentally imparts life to the dead soul, is the means by which the saints are conducted to glory. Hence the importance of having the word of Christ to dwell in us richly. Col. iii. 16. We may refer also to John xvii. 17. Every advance in sanctification through the truth is a step taken in the way that leads to eternal life.

II. *How Christians are to hold forth the word of life.* The idea is that the word of life is to be made prominent. It is to be conspicuously exhibited. The influence of the gospel depends materially on its being thus held forth. But how is it to be done?

1. *By a baptismal profession of faith in Christ, the Author of the gospel.* For such a profession all are qualified who have by the gospel been made subjects of spiritual life. In baptism they profess faith in Christ, they commemorate his burial and resurrection, and in emblem they set forth their personal death to sin, and resurrection to a new life.

This death to sin having occurred by means of the gospel, the word of life, which is the gospel, is held forth in baptism, which emblematically declares the believer's death to sin. Whenever baptism is administered to a believer, there is symbolical exhibition of the power of the gospel. The obligation to make this exhibition is both solemn and delightful.

2. *By church organization.* According to the gospel, baptized believers are embodied and organized into local churches. These churches are to maintain the worship of God. By so doing they hold forth the word of life. They are to sustain an evangelical ministry, exercise proper discipline, and celebrate the death of their Lord at his table. In these ways they hold forth the word of life.

3. *By living according to the gospel.* All other methods of holding forth the word of life are defective in the absence

of this. The power of the gospel to change the heart and regulate the life must be exhibited. The world cannot see the hearts of Christians, and how is the world to know that their hearts have been changed? The proof is to be furnished by the conformity of the lives of Christians to the requirements of the gospel. Every church should be an epistle of Christ, known and read by all men. Note well 2 Cor. iii. 3.

4. *By sending it to those who have it not.* This directs our attention to the work of missions. In these days, when all parts of the world are in telegraphic connection, all missions are virtually one. Every church is constitutionally a missionary society, and must see that the word of life is held forth at home and abroad. It must be held forth from the equator to the poles. The churches of the living God have in their custody the bread of life, and they must distribute it to earth's starving millions. How delightful would it be to see these millions feasted at the banquet of salvation! How gladly should Christians hold forth the word of life!

SAINTS IN GOD'S HAND.

All his saints are in thy hand.—Deut. xxxiii. 3.

Without introductory remarks, I at once inquire—

I. *Who are saints?* They are children of God by regeneration. They are "born of the Spirit," "born again," "new creatures," "created in Christ Jesus unto good works."

II. *Saints are in God's hand.* It may be said that all God's creatures are in his hand; but the saints are so in a peculiar sense. This will appear if we consider—

1. *They are in his loving hand.* His is the hand of a Father, and surely he loves those whom he has made his

children in so costly a manner, even through the incarnation and death of his own Son.

2. *They are in his guiding hand.* Well is it for them that they are not left to their own guidance. They know not the way in which they should go. They know not what is best for them.

3. *They are in his protecting hand.* How greatly they need protection! They need protection from themselves, protection from the evil influences of the world, and from the snares of Satan. His hand is stretched forth for their defence.

4. *They are in his chastening hand.* He chastens them with the paternal reluctance exemplified in a wise earthly father. Lam. iii. 33. His love prompts the application of the chastening rod. Heb. xii. 5–11.

5. *They are in his sustaining hand.* He holds them up otherwise they would sink beneath the waves of sorrow. The hour of death comes apace. How greatly will they need divine support in that hour when all human helpers fail!

REMARKS.

1. Are you one of the saints of God?

II. If so, remember, for your comfort, in whose hand you are.

BRINGING SINNERS TO JESUS.

And he brought him to Jesus.—John i. 42.

John the Baptist came to prepare a people for the Lord, and he loved to commend the Lord to the people prepared for him. More than once he said, "Behold the Lamb of God." These words, a sort of exclamatory command, were addressed at one time to two of his disciples, and they immediately followed Jesus. One of these disciples was Andrew, the brother of Peter. What did he do? He found Peter and said, "We have found the Messias." Not satisfied with telling Peter about Jesus, he brought him to Jesus. In this case there was physical movement, a bodily approach to the Saviour. This is impossible now. Still there is a sense in which sinners should be brought to Christ. They must be brought to him or perish. The present subject is—

BRINGING SINNERS TO JESUS.

The first thing claiming our attention is:

I. *Why should sinners be brought to Jesus.*

This should be done for such reasons as the following:

1. *Because they need salvation.* This necessity grows out of the fact that they are sinners. Sin is a terrible evil. It is a transgression of the divine law. It is treason against the government of God. It is an attempt to thwart his plans and purposes. It disturbs the harmony of the moral universe. It excites, and it is the only thing that excites, the wrath of God. Sinners are involved in the consequences of sin. These consequences, unless arrested, must be eternal. Guilt and condemnation are among these consequences, and also alienation from God. Do not sinners need salvation?

2. *Because there is salvation in Jesus alone.* What says Peter, the man whom Andrew brought to Christ? Years after, he spoke those words: "Neither is there salvation in any other: for there is none other name under heaven given among men, whereby we must be saved." Acts iv. 12. Why is there salvation in Christ alone? Because through him alone can the consequences of sin be arrested and removed. The great atoning transaction of Calvary provides for canceling guilt and reversing the sentence of condemnation. Christ bare our sins in his own body on the tree. 1 Peter ii. 24. This explains the whole matter. The cross, too, provides for overcoming the alienation I have referred to. Out of

Christ, where will you find salvation? Could you make the tour of the universe, going from world to world, you would find no salvation apart from Jesus.

3. *Because he promises to save all who are brought to him.* The anxious sinner might say, "I need salvation, and it must be in Jesus alone; but if his power is not exerted, what then? Has he made any promises?" Trembling soul, yes, yes. Here are his words: "Come unto me, all ye that labour and are heavy laden, and I will give you rest." "Him that cometh to me I will in no wise cast out." Matt. xi. 28; John vi. 37. To inspire perfect confidence in his promises he says: "Heaven and earth shall pass away, but my words shall not pass away." Matt. xxiv. 35.

3. *Because he has saved all who have been brought to him.* To this hour he has rejected none. He saved sinners before he died, by virtue of his prospective atonement; he saved the penitent thief while he was dying; and he has been saving sinners ever since he died. It has ever been his pleasure to exert his saving power, and in so doing he has performed his promises. I have surely given valid reasons why sinners should be brought to Jesus.

II. *Those who have been brought to Jesus should bring others to him.*

This will be seen if we consider that—

1. *They are one with him.* Brought to him, all their interests are merged in his. They have no interests apart from his. He came into the world to save sinners, and they must indorse his object by laboring to save sinners too. They are his representatives in the world, and how can they fitly represent him unless they bring sinners to him, that he may save them?

2. *This is contemplated in their conversion.* They are not made Christians merely that they may get to heaven, but that they may take others with them. How many were converted

to God through the apostles! and these converts engaged in the work of converting others, and they of others. This is the most practical, the most beneficial, the most sensible, and the most Scriptural apostolic succession the world ever saw, or ever will see. Let it never be forgotten that every sinner who has been brought to Jesus should do what he can to bring other sinners to him.

3. *In no other way can Christians show a proper estimation of Jesus as their Saviour.* They may say and do a hundred other things, but they can never prove their exalted appreciation of Christ so well as by bringing sinners to him for salvation. Those who love Jesus wish others to love him. Those who have been saved by him are anxious for others to be saved. The grace magnified in saving them they desire to see magnified in saving others. No Christian is in a normal state who is not employed in bringing sinners to Jesus.

III. *How may Christians bring sinners to Jesus?*

1. *By talking favorably of him.* They should earnestly and lovingly recommend him as a Saviour. Suppose you had been sick almost to death, and your physician had restored you to perfect health: what would you do if you saw others diseased as you had been? Would you, could you, be silent? You would talk about your physician. So talk of Jesus, the Physician of souls. Say without a doubt that he can cure any morally diseased sinner, because he has cured you. Andrew talked to Peter about the Messiah, and Peter willingly went to Jesus.

2. *By holiness of life.* When religion shows its power to make its professed friends what they say they are, it always benefits sinners. They are ready to say that there is a reality in the religion which makes bad men good, which renders the covetous liberal, which enables the irritable man to control his temper, and which places earthly concerns in subordination to eternal interests.

3. *By showing that they are joyful in the work of Jesus.* Some professed Christians act as if they considered it a hardship to serve Christ. You must let the world see that his service is your joy and your delight. If you go about morose and gloomy, like a Pharisee on a fast-day, you will repel sinners from Jesus. They will not be attracted by such a specimen of piety as that. "Rejoice in the Lord always."

4. *By prayer to God for their salvation.* The success of all effort depends on God. No sinner is willing to be brought to Jesus till made willing in the day of God's power. Prayer recognizes this fact and looks upward. Prayer avails much. It takes hold of God's strength and thus allies man's weakness to divine omnipotence. Pray without ceasing.

REMARKS.

I. Bringing sinners to Jesus is a great work; greater than founding a kingdom or an empire.

II. Will you not be more earnest in this work?

III. Sinners must be brought to Jesus soon or never.

IV. O sinners, be brought, be led to Jesus now.

A GOOD SOLDIER OF JESUS CHRIST.

Thou therefore endure hardness, as a good soldier of Jesus Christ.—2 Tim. ii. 3.

Christians are variously designated in the Scriptures. In many passages, as in the text, they are referred to under military imagery, and represented as soldiers in the army of "the Captain of their salvation." They are required to "put on the whole armour of God," that they may "withstand in the evil day." They are exhorted to "fight the good fight of faith," and to "lay hold on eternal life." The text invites us to contemplate the character of—

A GOOD SOLDIER OF JESUS CHRIST.

In answer to the question, Who is a good soldier of Jesus Christ? it may be said:

I. *A regenerate person.* In literal warfare a bad man may be a good soldier. This was the opinion of the great Napoleon, and he cared but little for the moral character of those who fought under his banner. In Christian warfare the good soldier is the good man, and there is no evangelical goodness apart from regeneration. The heart needs to be changed The natural man must be born again, so as to become a spiritual man. John iii. 7; 2 Cor. v. 17. Without this birth from above there may be nominal soldiers in the hosts of Immanuel, but there can be no good soldier of Jesus Christ.

2. *One who makes the will of Christ his will.* This coincidence of will is one of the blessed effects of regeneration. "What wilt thou have me to do?" was the first question of Saul of Tarsus, when he felt the impulses of spiritual life in his soul. What would a literal army become if the will of the commander was not supreme and imperative? It would soon be an irresponsible mob. Christ as the Captain of Salvation issues his orders, and the good soldier knows nothing but to obey. In his regeneration there is an internal surrender of his will to the will of Christ; and in his public enlistment, in his baptism, there is an external surrender, a declaration of allegiance to Christ, and a promise to do his will.

III. *A good soldier of Jesus Christ has true courage.* A coward soldier is a contradiction in terms. A soldier's heart beats not in a coward. The Christian soldier is strong in the Lord and in the power of his might. Apart from the Lord he has no strength. His contest is a "fight of faith," and faith allies the believer to his Lord, so that he can avail himself of his Lord's strength. He therefore goes forth courageously, and his confidence in his Commander is the inspiration of his courage.

IV. *A good soldier of Christ endures hardness patiently.* This is the injunction of the text, "endure hardness." If the literal soldier enters on military life supposing it to be a life of ease, he soon finds out his mistake. The camp, the march, the battle-field, the hospital, all remind him of the hardships of war. The Christian soldier has privations, trials, and burdens to bear. Jesus says to his disciples, "In the world ye shall have tribulation." John xvi. 33. Paul writes to the Philippians, "For unto you it is given in the behalf of Christ, not only to believe on him, but also to suffer for his sake." Phil. i. 29. Peter records these words: "Beloved, think it not strange concerning the fiery trial which is to try you, as though some strange thing happened unto you." 1 Peter iv. 12. Not to be called to endure hardness would be the strange thing, for the enduring of hardness is inseparable from the Christian soldier's life. This hardness the good soldier of Jesus Christ bears patiently and even cheerfully for the sake of his great Leader and Commander.

V. *A good soldier of Christ tries to get others to enlist.* This, to say the least, is not always the case with literal soldiers. Having experienced the hardships of war, they often advise others not to adopt the life of a soldier. Not so with good soldiers of Christ. They desire recruits for Immanuel's army, and the better soldiers they are, the more anxious they are to have accessions made to his hosts. They devote themselves personally to the work of entreating sinners to abandon the hosts of Satan and come over on the Lord's side. No man is a good soldier of Jesus Christ who does not try to get others to become Christ's soldiers.

VI. *A good soldier of Christ expects to triumph over all the enemies of his salvation.* He goes not forth to battle trembling under the paralysis of fear, but buoyant with hope. He remembers that of Christian soldiers it is written, "we are more than conquerors through him that loved us." Rom.

viii. 37 He hears the inspiring words, "Thanks be to God, which giveth us the victory through our Lord Jesus Christ." 1 Cor. xv. 57. The Christian soldier, "strong in the Lord and in the power of his might" expects to see every foe subdued, even death, the last enemy, destroyed; and expects to sing a song of triumph which God will delight to hear.

REMARKS.

I. Are you a good soldier of Jesus Christ?

II. If you are his enemy, what an appalling prospect is before you!

III. Kiss the Son, lest he be angry, and ye perish from the way.

SPIRITUAL POWER.

But ye shall receive power, after that the Holy Ghost is come upon you.—Acts i. 8.

Jesus had risen from the dead, and had given his apostles infallible proofs of his resurrection. Having instructed them for forty days concerning the kingdom of God, the time of his ascension was at hand. It seems that in his last interview with his disciples, they wished to know whether the kingdom was to be restored to Israel. He rebuked their curiosity, saying: "It is not for you to know the times or the seasons." Acts i. 7. He, however, told them what was of far greater personal interest to them. "But ye shall receive power." This is a repetition of the idea expressed in Luke xxiv. 49. The topic of the hour is—

SPIRITUAL POWER.

That we may understand the nature of this power, let us consider some of the most important elements:

I. *Experimental knowledge of the grace of God.* Piety is

a thing of the heart, and therefore a matter of experience. The most extensive theoretical knowledge does not involve the power of which I speak. Paul refers to knowing "the grace of God in truth." This is the knowledge I mean. It differs from speculative knowledge of divine things as much as knowledge of food, gained by eating, differs from knowledge of it gained in all other ways. There is a volume of sense in the words "Taste and see," "Come and see." No one can properly use these words who has not the knowledge of experience. He must know God as Lawgiver, and himself as a transgressor. He must know himself as a sinner, and Christ as the Saviour. He must be able to say, "I know that the gospel is true because I have felt its power." The greater this knowledge in any Christian, the greater is his spiritual power.

II. *Vigorous faith.* I use the term faith in its fullest sense.

1. *Faith in God.* There must be the influential belief that Jehovah is the living God whose eye is upon us. We must live and act as in his sight—as seeing the Invisible One.

2. *Faith in unseen and eternal things.* In the only definition of faith we have in the Bible it is termed the evidence, or confident assurance, of things not seen. Without this faith there is no spiritual power. Without it the world sweeps every thing before it.

3. *Faith in Christ.* This faith makes the believer cling to his Lord as all his salvation.

4. *Faith in the success of effort in the Lord's cause.* No man is prepared to engage in a work unless he believes it will succeed. Unbelief destroys expectation and dishonors God. What does Jesus say? Matt. ix. 29; xvii. 20; Mark ix. 23. Unbelief is a great obstacle. Matt. xiii. 58. Faith enlists all the energies of the soul; unbelief paralyzes them.

III. *Fervent love.* I use also the term love in its enlarged sense, as including:

1. *Love to God,* which puts the soul in sympathy with his purposes.

2. *Love to Christ* and the interests of his kingdom.

3. *Love to saints* for Christ's sake.

4. *Love to impenitent sinners.* Love is an element of great spiritual power. To reach sinners, in our efforts for their salvation we must intensely love their souls. Love can find a way to the heart when nothing else can. It has much more to do with Christian usefulness than has talent or learning. Without it all effort will be formal and spasmodic. There will be no heart in it.

IV. *Ardent and untiring zeal.* He who has the power of which I speak is most deeply impressed with the importance of the work in which he is engaged. There is therefore a zealous and an enthusiastic consecration to it. Every thing else appears trivial. There seems to be but one thing to do. The glory of God in the salvation of men is the all-absorbing object. Zeal is therefore ardent, and because ardent, untiring. Difficulties and trials do not extinguish it. These are prominent elements of spiritual power.

V. *This power comes from the Holy Spirit.* What says the text? True, the Spirit supplied the apostles with the miraculous power of speaking with tongues. I refer, however, to such power as has been described, and which all Christians should possess and may possess. This power is of the Spirit. It can be produced by no discipline physical or mental, by none of the appliances of philosophy. "Endued with power from on high," is the language of Jesus. The power comes from on high. It is not an earthly power. It comes from above. It puts heaven and earth in communication. Ponder the elements of this power, and you will see that the agency of the Holy Spirit alone is adequate to its creation. Who but the Spirit can give experimental knowledge of the grace of God? Who but he can inspire vigorous faith, fervent love, and ardent zeal? The power of which I speak is inseparable from eminent piety; and piety, in its lowest type, is the product of the Spirit. Much more, in its highest form, does it come from the Divine Spirit.

REMARKS.

I. Spiritual power is the great need of Christians in this day.

II. We should cultivate a sense of dependence on the Holy Spirit.

III. We should earnestly pray for the Spirit. See Luke xi. 13.

EXERCISING UNTO GODLINESS.

Exercise thyself [rather] unto godliness.—1 Tim. iv. 7.

The world is full of exertion, another name for exercise. We live in an active, busy age. Effort is the order of the day, and there is no disposition to suspend the order. There is activity wherever there is a prospect of utility and, alas, in many cases where there is no such prospect. There is much unprofitable and injurious action. The great thing is to have action properly directed. God has made his creatures for action. Unless the bodily powers are exercised they are injured. So of the intellectual and moral faculties. The text refers to exercise. My topic is—

EXERCISING UNTO GODLINESS.

An important question arises:

I. *What is godliness?* It is piety, it is consecration to God Psalm iv. 3. But to be more specific—

I. *It has to do with the affections of the heart.* It is a dictate of reason as well as revelation that piety cannot exist without a proper state of heart. Who are the ungodly? Those whose hearts are so under the dominion of sin that they do not love God. In a destitution of love to God sin has its origin, and its full possibilities of development are unknown. Here is its beginning. If so, the beginning of godliness is to be looked for in a heart that loves God. You look in vain for such a heart till you find one that is changed. Love to God is the fruit of regeneration. 1 John iv. 7. This change makes the new creature. 2 Cor. v. 17. It creates a new disposition, and it places the affections on new objects. It inspires a relish for spiritual things and an appreciation of their excellence. The subjects of this change love God and cherish his views of sin and holiness.

2. *It has to do with the words of the mouth.* We are prone to forget what importance the Scriptures attach to words. What does Jesus say? See Matt. xii. 36, 37. That godliness has to do with the tongue, we may see from Eph. iv. 15, 29; Col. iii. 8; James i. 26; 1 Peter ii. 1; iii. 10. The mouth is not to be desecrated. But this negative godliness will not suffice; there must be a consecration of the power of speech. Piety is sadly incomplete without it.

3. *It has to do with the actions of the life.* Affections, words, and actions, are all of man. They are expansible into everything that pertains to him. The religion of Jesus is eminently practical. Luke vi. 46; Phil. ii. 13; Titus ii. 11–14. Godliness ever includes the conformity of the life to the will of God. It begins with the heart; but out of the heart are the issues of life.

II. *Exercise unto godliness is necessary.* The word translated exercise in the text is very expressive. In proof of this I need only say that it belongs to the same family of words in which *gymnasium* is found. The extent of the exercise and discipline of the Greek gymnasiums was so great as to be nearly incredible. Imagine Paul to be thinking of the Grecian youths exercising themselves with respect to athletic games, and saying to young Timothy: "Exercise thyself [rather] unto godliness." What does this command imply?

1. *Uncompromising war against sin.* Sin is the opposite of godliness. You cannot exercise yourself unto godliness without waging a war of extermination against sin.

a. Sins of the heart. How numerous and subtle they are! We are in more danger of committing these sins because the eyes of others cannot see them. Sins of the heart include hatred, envy, jealousy, hypocrisy, covetousness, wrath, love of the world, dissatisfaction with providence, motives tinctured with impurity. These may be regarded as the Christian's mortal foes. He or they must die in the conflict. The war is internecine. Hatred, envy, and jealousy must be supplanted by love; hypocrisy, by sincerity; covetousness, by liberality. What searchings of the heart are necessary! And after they are made, we have to pray: "Cleanse thou me from secret faults." The heart must be kept with all diligence. Sins must be detected in their lurking places, dragged out, and slain before the Lord. We must, if need be, resist unto blood, striving against sin.

b. Sins of the tongue. How difficult to control the tongue! Perfection is ascribed to the man who offends not in word. James iii. 2. Do you say, discouraged Christian, that you cannot be perfect in this sense? You must *exercise* yourself. The best way to control the tongue is to control the heart.

c. Sins of the life. Avoid the wrong and pursue the right. You are subjected not only to the scrutiny of men and angels, but to the inspection of God. Let your conduct be as becomes the gospel of Christ. "Exercise thyself unto godliness." If you fail a thousand times to come up fully to the standard of duty, still try. *Exercise*, EXERCISE, EXERCISE thyself unto godliness, and remember that in doing so you wage an uncompromising war with sin.

2. *Diligent cultivation of the Christian graces.* These

graces are in inseparable connection with godliness. In proportion to their growth, godliness increases. Cherish faith by thinking of those things in God, in Christ, in the Holy Spirit, in the gospel, that are adapted to inspire confidence. "Keep yourselves in the love of God." Supply the fire of love on the altar of the heart with appropriate fuel, that the flame may be steady and bright. Stimulate zeal by reflecting how God will be glorified in the increase of your personal spirituality, in the edification of your fellow-Christians, and in the salvation of impenitent sinners. Animate hope by contemplating the promises, and the bright prospects which these promises open to view. Deepen humility by considering your unworthiness resulting from your unfaithfulness. Let patience have its perfect work; and in order to this imbibe the spirit of your Saviour, who was meek and lowly in heart, and whose symbol was the lamb. This cultivation of the graces will require strenuous exercise.

3. *The highest possible attainments in godliness.* What spiritual dwarfs are most Christians! How few attain the stature of men! Still the possibilities of Christian attainment are wonderful, as may be seen from Eph. iii. 14–20. Why are not these possibilities more frequently illustrated? It is owing to a failure to obey the command of the text. We do not rise without effort to the lofty heights of spiritual life. There is no such thing as elevation by accident to these heights. "Exercise thyself," is the law of spiritual advancement. The blessing of God rests most abundantly on those who with most earnestness and perseverance exercise themselves unto godliness.

REMARK.

We may learn from this subject what is truly noble in human endeavor, namely, exercise unto godliness.

THE CHRISTIAN VOCATION.

I therefore, the prisoner of the Lord, beseech you that ye walk worthy of the vocation wherewith ye are called.—Eph. iv. 1.

A man's vocation, or calling, is his profession or occupation. The practice of medicine is the calling of the physician. It is his business. The vocation of the lawyer is the practice of the law. It devolves on him to apply the great principles of justice as embodied in the system of law. The calling of the merchant is his occupation with the affairs of merchandise. The farmer's vocation has to do with agriculture. The Christian has a calling which will now engage our attention.

THE CHRISTIAN VOCATION.

I notice—

I. *The nature of this vocation.* What theologians have termed "effectual calling," is regeneration. This is evident from Rom. viii. 30. Of this calling much may be said. I attempt a summary view. I say then that the calling is—

1. *From God.* 1 Thess. ii. 12; 1 Peter v. 10.
2. *According to his purpose.* Rom. viii. 28.
3. *From darkness to light.* 1 Peter ii. 9.
4. *To liberty.* Gal. v. 13.
5. *To fellowship with Christ.* 1 Cor. i. 9.
6. *To holiness.* 1 Thess. iv. 7.
7. *To eternal life.* 1 Tim. vi. 12.

From these particulars we see that matters of the greatest importance, and interests of infinite magnitude, are involved in this vocation. Well is it termed a high calling, and a heavenly calling. It as far transcends all earthly callings, as the light of the sun exceeds that of the glow-worm. It calls from all that is low and sinful and miserable, to all that is high and holy and glorious. It calls from earth to heaven. It calls from these mortal scenes to the bright realms of immortal glory.

II. *Walking worthy of this vocation.* Walk, as the word is often used in Scripture, means to act, to live, to conduct one's self. It is assumed in the text that there is a deportment consistent with the Christian calling, and therefore worthy of it. What kind of a deportment is this? It implies many things, of which I name the following:

1. *That we uniformly act as Christians.* We know that the term Christian is derived from the proper name Christ. A Christian therefore should not only have the mind of Christ, but live as he lived. 1 John ii. 6. It is said that he has left us an example that we should follow his steps—act as he acted. Our feelings revolt, if in thought we associate the name of Christ with falsehood, fraud, levity, fretfulness, oppression, injustice in any of its forms. We mentally say, the inconsistency is too monstrous to think of. Christians should be like Christ in exemplifying all that is right and just and good. They must not only practice the moral virtues, but transform them into Christian graces. But I have used the word *uniformly*—uniformly act as Christians. It is easy to do this on Sunday when you go to church, or to prayer-meeting during the week. We must live religiously everywhere, at home and abroad, in our business and other occupations. This is what is needed: a religion to sanctify the relations and the pursuits of life, turning all our activities into a consecrated channel. The Christian who lives in a manner worthy of his vocation, does right because it is right, and because Christ requires him to do so.

2. *That we practically regard verses two and three.* I mean the verses following the text. With all *lowliness.* Humility is inculcated. Among the Greeks this was considered meanness, abjectness, baseness. Humility is a Christian grace. Jesus was lowly in heart. How much there is to make us humble! Let us think what we *were*, what we *are*, and what we *hope* to be. *Meekness.* This term denotes the disposition

with which we receive afflictions from God and injuries from men. In the former case the heart is crushed, but does not murmur; in the latter, there is no retaliation, no spirit of revenge. *Long-suffering.* This means not only that we are to suffer, but to suffer long with those persons and things that put our patience to the test. *Forbearing one another in love.* The forbearance can be exercised only in love. *Keeping the unity of the Spirit.* There must be earnest effort to do this, to maintain the unity created by the Holy Spirit. Unity results from union of hearts. *Bond of peace.* A peaceful temper binding all hearts together.

3. *That we labor for the salvation of sinners.* No one deserves to be called a Christian who does not desire that sinners may be saved, and no one walks worthy of the Christian vocation who does not put forth effort to accomplish this object. There is nothing in which the Christian acts more consistently with his profession than in leading sinners to Christ.

4. *That we live as pilgrims on earth.* Christians are not of the world, are only passing through it, and will soon be out of it. If so, heaven is very near to them. My brother, my sister, you may be in heaven in a month, in a week, in a day. Act under this impression, and you will walk worthy of your vocation. Do you think that you would violate your baptismal vows to-day if you expected to see the mansicns of glory to-morrow? No, you would adorn the doctrine of God. Living as pilgrims, you would walk worthy of your high and holy vocation.

REMARKS.

I. How have you walked in time past?

II. Christian usefulness has an important connection with consistent Christian deportment.

III. This shows why there is not a large measure of Christian usefulness.

PERSONAL AND FAMILY RELIGION.

But as for me and my house, we will serve the Lord.—*Joshua* xxiv. 15.

These words were spoken amid solemn circumstances. Joshua said: "This day I am going the way of all the earth." He gathered all the tribes of Israel to Shechem, and gave them a summary of Old Testament history from the father of Abraham down to the time at which he spoke. In view of all that God had done for them, he exhorted them to fear and serve him. He submitted the matter to their choice. Joshua knew that voluntary service alone would be acceptable to God. Hence, he said, "Choose you this day whom ye will serve." "But as for me and my house we will serve the Lord." Theme—

PERSONAL AND FAMILY RELIGION.

Let us observe—

I. *How this religion is designated.* It is called serving the Lord. What is implied in this service?

1. *Conformity of the servant's will to the will of the Master.* It is characteristic of those who do not serve God that their wills are in conflict with his will. There is on their part rebellious collision. They are not willing for God to have his way. They are determined to do as they please. The essence of sin is to be found in the lack of harmony between the will of God and the will of his rational creatures. There should be no clashing of wills in the universe. Every other will should move in sweet accord with the will of God. If these views are correct, the service of which I speak implies regeneration, which changes the will as well as the affections. Psalm cx. 3. Every subject of this gracious change says, "Thy will, O Lord, be done." This conformity of will to the will of God secures *voluntary* service, and no other service is acceptable to him. The *compulsory* element does not enter into the service that God requires.

2. *Supreme love for the Master.* On this point, as well as on the preceding one, we see how literal service differs from the service of God. Go, in thought, to the slaves of Greece or Rome, or anywhere else, and you will seldom find love for masters. When found, it would not be an essential of slavery, but something entirely accidental. So also of hired servants. But the servants of God love him supremely. This is an essential, it is the central element of the service rendered to him. Without it all service would be "as sounding brass or tinkling cymbal." There is no substitute for this love. Psalm lxxiii. 25; Luke xiv. 26.

3. *Obedience to the Master's commands.* The servant of the Lord has nothing left to his discretion. He is not permitted to say whether he will obey or not. Nor can he make selections from the commands. The only proper question for him is: "What am I required to do?" He has no right to ask the reason of a requirement. It may be best for him not to know. If the Master gives the reason, well; if not, well. We have the model of perfect service in heaven, in Matt. vi. 10.

4. *Devotion to the Master's interests.* The servant has no separate interests; or, at any rate, has no right to have any. He is the Master's, and everything pertaining to him is the Master's also. The more faithful the servant, the more devoted he is to the Master's interests. The servant is to abound in the work of the Master. It is not his work, but the Master's. It is the Master's cause, and consecration to this cause is serving the Lord.

The characteristics of this service have to do—

II. *With persons and families.* "As for me," says Joshua. Religion has its beginning with individuals. In its internal aspect it is a spiritual creation in individual hearts. "Every one that loveth is born of God." 1 John iv. 7. In this new birth, piety has its origin. If there is family religion, i is preceded by personal religion. Otherwise it cannot exist. In a Christian family, parents must be individually pious, and children likewise. The father's piety cannot be placed to the account of the mother, nor can children inherit piety from parents. Grace does not run in the blood, and is not therefore transmissible by ancestors to their posterity. Religion is intensely personal in its beginnings, and indeed never lays aside its personal aspect; but, according to the text, it has a family aspect. "As for me and my house, we will serve the Lord." There are strong reasons why the Lord should be served in families. Consider the following:

1. *God has appointed the family institution.* We are told that he "setteth the solitary in families." Psalm lviii. 6. The family constitution is the best preservation of social order. There is no social order without it. The union of husband and wife in marriage is the basis of the family organization. Parents are required to train their children "in the nurture and admonition of the Lord." Eph. vi. 4. Children must obey their parents in the Lord. Domestics should come under the beneficial influences of the family circle. God, having appointed the family institution, is ever to be recognized in it. Alas for those families that withhold this recognition!

2. *Families are dependent on God.* If there is personal dependence, there is family dependence. If there is personal obligation to serve God, there is family obligation; and it should be acknowledged by families in the joint service they render to the Lord.

3. *Families receive blessings from God.* How numerous these blessings! How sweet the comforts of home! How precious the advantages enjoyed in a well-regulated family! Must not God be served in such a family? Must there not be a family altar, from which, morning and evening, the incense of praise and prayer shall ascend? Can any head of

a family say that he and his house serve the Lord, unless family worship is maintained?

4. *The influence of families on civil governments and on churches is great.* The virtue and intelligence essential to good government must be fostered in families. If neglected, ruin will, sooner or later, come on any country under any form of government. Religion in churches will be very much what it is in families. The type of family piety will be reproduced in church piety. Church piety, whether earnest or lukewarm, will ordinarily be a development of the kind of piety exemplified in the home.

REMARKS.

I. Have you this *personal* religion?

II. What is the state of religion in your *family?*

THE CHOICE THAT MOSES MADE.

By faith Moses, when he was come to years, refused to be called the son of Pharaoh's daughter: choosing rather to suffer affliction with the people of God than to enjoy the pleasures of sin for a season: esteeming the reproach of Christ greater riches than the treasures in Egypt; for he had respect to the recompense of the reward.—Heb. xi. 24-26.

Among the remarkable men of whom the Bible gives us information, there was no one more remarkable than Moses. The preservation of his infant life was so obviously providential as to appear almost miraculous. Rescued from a watery grave, he was adopted by the daughter of Pharaoh, and instructed in all the departments of Egyptian knowledge He became the legislator of the Israelites, led them out of the land of bondage, conducted them through the Red Sea, through the wilderness, stood on Pisgah, saw the land of promise, but did not enter into it.

The laws which Moses enacted under the direction of God, have made their impression on the world. Their influence is certainly co-extensive with civilization. The text has reference to a very interesting period of his life. My topic will be—

THE CHOICE THAT MOSES MADE.

That this choice may be rightly appreciated, it is well to notice—

I. *What Moses refused.* The things he refused were the three following:

1. *To be called the son of Pharaoh's daughter.* He had been adopted, and no doubt received an education suitable to the relation he sustained to the king's family. Whether he was heir apparent to the throne, as some suppose, we cannot say; but his position was one of importance and dignity. To refuse to recognize his relation to the king's daughter was a voluntary surrender of what the world would call brilliant hopes and prospects. The word refused is suggestive. It seems to imply that attempts were made to influence Moses to avail himself of the great advantages so easily within his reach. Possibly he rejected the tearful entreaties of the queen's daughter. His refusal was decided, inflexible.

2. *To enjoy the pleasures of sin for a season.* It is here implied that there is pleasure in sin. This, owing to man's vitiated moral taste, is true. Probably there is more pleasure at court than anywhere else. Royalty has every wish gratified that can be gratified. Moses, knowing the pleasures of the Egyptian court to be sinful, refused to participate in them. He knew, also, that these pleasures were but "for a season." Let men of the world, and let the daughters of folly and fashion, remember that "the pleasures of sin" are temporary.

3. *To avail himself of the treasures in Egypt.* The inference is that Moses might have been rich. The wealth of Egypt at that time was immense, comparatively inexhaustible; but Moses cared not for it. The insane purpose to be

rich has ruined multitudes. Some say they do not regard wealth, but if they could, like Moses, have it by choosing it, they would not hesitate. He refused. Strange refusal, was it not? He refused wealth, as well as honor and pleasure—these three things being termed by Richard Baxter, "the worldly man's trinity."

The refusal of Moses emphasizes his choice.

II. *What he chose.* The text mentions two things:

1. *To suffer affliction with the people of God.* The Israelites, during the early and middle life of Moses, were a nation of slaves. In them was verified the prophetic word to Abraham that his seed should be brought into bondage and suffer grievous oppression. When Moses came forth to assume the leadership of the Israelites, they were groaning under their burdens and hopeless of relief. They were looked upon by the proud Egyptians with contempt and disdain. But they were the people of God. Moses identified himself with them. They were afflicted, but he was willing, and even preferred, to suffer affliction with them. He refused pleasure and chose affliction—a course utterly at war with the practice of worldly men. There is nothing desirable in affliction itself, but there may be considerations connected with it which make it wise to choose it and bear it with meekness and patience. Thus it was with Moses. He chose affliction with the people of God, identifying his interest and destiny with theirs.

2. *The reproach of Christ.* It is possible that when the Epistle to the Hebrews was written, the phrase "reproach of Christ," meant all the ridicule, contempt, and scorn that a man suffered for being a servant of God. If so, Paul means—for I believe that Paul wrote this Epistle—that Moses esteemed the disgrace which wicked men associated with piety as of more value than riches, "greater riches than the treasures in Egypt." Observe, not piety itself, but the reproach incurred by its friends, of more value than the greatest

wealth. Of what infinite value then is piety when the reproach of it is worth so much! As to the refusal and choice of Moses, we cannot say that they resulted from youth ful enthusiasm, for the text tells us that they occurred "when he was come to years." His mind was mature. He had the best reasons for what he did. This leads me to say—

III. *His faith accounts for the course he pursued.* "By faith" he refused, and "by faith" he chose. He believed that the Messiah would descend from the persecuted, down-trodden Israelites. This made him willing to merge his fortunes into theirs. He chose to be identified with a people out of whom should come the great Deliverer. In addition to this specific item of faith, Moses had the general faith defined in the first verse of this chapter as "the substance of things hoped for, the evidence of things not seen." This shows why "he had respect to the recompense of the reward." The substance of what he hoped for was "the recompense of the reward." His faith made the recompense of the reward, not a shadow, but a substantial reality.

Faith is the evidence, the confident assurance, of the existence of things not seen. While the bodily senses bring us into contact with the natural world, faith brings us into contact with the invisible world, and thus its realities impress the mind and the heart. Moses believed in an unseen God, "for he endured as seeing him who is invisible." He acted as if he saw God looking into the transactions of his life, and the secrets of his heart. He believed in an unseen heaven, an unseen hell, an unseen eternity. This is the explanation of his refusal and of his choice. In view of the magnitude of eternal things, how unspeakably paltry appeared the advantages of his adoption, the pleasures of a court, and the wealth of Egypt! How did all things earthly dwindle into their proper insignificance! Great is the power of faith, and this power found a living illustration in Moses. We see how his refusal and his choice resulted by a sublime necessity from his faith.

REMARKS.

I. Moses was truly wise. It would have been the greatest folly for him to have transposed his refusal and his choice.

II. Are you like Moses, in looking, not at the things which are seen and temporary, but at those which are unseen and eternal?

III. The stronger our faith, the more we think of our souls, of heaven, of eternity.

THE VALUE OF TRUTH.

Buy the truth, and sell it not.—Proverbs xxiii. 23.

We all know what truth is. It is a representation of things as they are. It is conformity to fact or reality; the opposite of error or falsehood. Truth is of great importance in all the realms of human investigation. The more important a subject, the more important the truth concerning it. An error in placing a decimal may involve serious consequences. Some of Sir Isaac Newton's calculations, it is said, were suspended for years, because errors had crept into them and vitiated the results. Truth in science is to be regarded. A mistake as to gravitation or chemical combinations may do great injury. A false view in mental philosophy may do untold harm. But in the realm of things spiritual, how much more valuable is truth! Here is seen its supreme preciousness; for it has to do with the soul, and salvation, and eternity. The text tells us what to do with truth—buy it and not sell it. My topic will be—

THE VALUE OF TRUTH.

It is of such value that it should be bought at any price, and sold at no price. I speak of human agency in buying or obtaining the truth.

I. *What is to be paid for it?* To possess it, something is to be done, and the something is the price to be paid. The constituent parts of the price may be considered the following:

1. *Requisite time.* To the acquisition of truth the necessary time must be given. It cannot be gained when all our time is given to other things. You may say that much of your time has to be spent otherwise. Be it so; still there is time to buy the truth. While engaged in other matters you may be seeking after truth. If this were not so, it is the part of wisdom to employ time most profitably. This is done by getting possession of truth.

2. *Earnest attention.* The requisite time must not only be given, but it must be improved by diligent, earnest attention. No feeble, languid desire for truth will do. It must be sought as men seek for "hid treasures." Prov. ii. 4. This they do with profound earnestness. So must we seek after truth.

3. *Perfect candor.* This is the opposite of prejudice and partiality. If there is prejudice against the truth there is a huge barrier in the way of gaining it. If there is partiality for one truth rather than another, the influence of such a state is unfavorable. Perfect candor is indispensable.

4. *Childlike docility.* This is closely connected with candor, but distinguishable from it. It is teachableness, willingness to learn. It implies a readiness to receive truth, no matter what it is, nor how strange it may be. This docility made itself vocal when it prompted the child Samuel to say, "Speak, Lord, for thy servant heareth."

II. *When is the truth sold.* Of course, selling the truth is a figurative transaction. That is to say, there is no literal sale. Yet the truth may be given up. This is done—

1. *When a proper estimate is not placed on it.* Undervaluing the truth is the first step toward giving it up. In the metaphorical language of the text, it is the first proposal to sell it.

2. *When error is permitted to usurp its place.* Whether permission is given thoughtlessly or with design, truth is sold.

3. *When it is held loosely with a view to avoid the charge of bigotry.* Many are afraid of this charge. They are guilty of moral cowardice. Their feeble hold of truth makes it easy to give it up, and they do give it up when they think occasion requires it. There is no bigotry in a zealous attachment to truth. Still with many the charge of bigotry is so much dreaded that they swerve from the truth. In these three ways men sell the truth.

III. *Why should we buy, and not sell the truth.* We have seen, in part at least, what it is to buy and to sell the truth. Now why should we do the one and not the other? I answer—

1. *Because of the value of truth.* If, as the text implies, truth should be bought at any price, for there is no limit; and sold at no price, for the prohibition is absolute, then it must possess great value. I speak now of truth in general. Of evangelical truth I may say with emphasis, that it possesses transcendent value. Its worth is seen in what it teaches—

a. Of God. It makes known his character, his will, his relation to us as Creator and Lawgiver, to whom we are under infinite obligations.

b. Of man. It answers the otherwise unanswerable questions, Whence came I? What am I? Whither do I go? It tells of man's condemnation and ruin, his guilty helplessness and helpless guilt.

c. Of salvation through Christ. It clearly makes known the fact that the only way of deliverance from sin and ruin is through the blood of the cross.

d. Of the way to live. We are to glorify God on the earth by doing good to our fellow-creatures.

e. Of triumph over death. This triumph is secured by the extraction of the sting of death through Christ. 1 Cor. xv. 54–57.

f. Of everlasting life in heaven. It tells of a blissful existence, immortal as the existence of God. Is there not infinite value in evangelical truth if it teaches these important things?

REMARKS.

I. Prize the truth more highly as the means of conversion and sanctification.

II. Error in the spiritual constitution is like poison in the physical constitution; its influence is evil and evil only.

III. Truth is so intolerant that it can make no compromise with error.

WISDOM BETTER THAN GOLD.

How much better is it to get wisdom than gold!—Proverbs xvi. 16.

Solomon was the wisest of men, and he had gold in abundance. He was therefore well qualified to form a judgment as to the comparative value of wisdom and gold. His judgment is expressed in the text. We must remember, however, that "all Scripture is given by inspiration of God." This being the case, the words before us are to be regarded as the declaration of God that wisdom is better than gold. There can then be no mistake about the matter. It will be our present business to consider the fact that—

WISDOM IS BETTER THAN GOLD.

My purpose requires me to—

I. *Define the terms gold and wisdom.*

1. *Gold.* It has from time immemorial been called one of the precious metals. This means that it possesses great value. It is precious because it answers the most important secular purposes. There is no earthly thing, within the limits of possibility, that cannot be accomplished by means of gold. Do you desire palatial mansions? Do you wish all sections of the country united by railroads? Would you have space

virtually annihilated by telegraph? Would you have the earth to disgorge its mineral deposits? Would you have majestic ships to sail over the sea? All these things can be done by means of gold, or its equivalent. Without gold the progress of civilization would be arrested. In short, without gold the face of the whole world must be changed. I recognize the claims of gold in calling it the representative of all earthly good.

2. *Wisdom.* Even the wisdom of this world is valuable. Often have the interests of nations been secured by the wisdom of statesmen. Wisdom is better than knowledge, for it turns knowledge to good account. Large measures of knowledge are often worthless in the absence of wisdom. I refer thus far to worldly wisdom. But Solomon uses the term wisdom in a higher sense, in which "the fear of the Lord is the beginning" of it. The fear of the Lord is so the beginning of wisdom that there is, without it, no wisdom connected with salvation. This wisdom is referred to in Job xxviii. 28, and in Psalm cxi. 10. It is declared in this Book of Proverbs to be "the principal thing." The fear of the Lord is reverence for his character and his authority. Into this reverence love enters as an essential element in union with fear, divesting fear of its slavish feature and substituting the filial feature.

II. *Why wisdom is better than gold.*

The following reasons may be assigned:

1. *It is suited to the nature of the soul.* Gold is not, for it cannot meet the cravings of the immortal mind. Who was ever made happy by gold? The largest amount of it does not confer happiness. Observe, the owners of gold may be happy; but it is something besides gold that renders them so. They have wisdom, another name for the religion of Jesus; and what does Jesus say in Matt. iv. 28; John iv. 14? See also what is said of wisdom in Proverbs iii. 17.

2 *It is connected with salvation.* There is no such connection between gold and salvation. A man may have no gold, and yet have the grace of God in his soul. The poor of this world may be rich in faith. All the gold of Ophir cannot procure salvation. The precious metal, so-called, is not current in the realm of grace. On the other hand, there is such a connection between wisdom and salvation that the latter is impossible without the former. "The fear of the Lord is the beginning of wisdom." Those only who fear the Lord are saved; and salvation is infinitely important. How deeply and vitally it involves our best, our eternal interests! The subject will appear a thousand times more important a thousand centuries hence than it does now. Salvation comprehends a change of heart, pardon of sin, adoption into the family of God, a life of consecration to his service, preparation for death, a glorious resurrection, and everlasting blessedness in heaven. With all these things wisdom has an essential connection, but gold has not. Gold cannot buy any of them. He who has wisdom, the true wisdom, will have them all. If so, is not wisdom better than gold? Does not its superiority appear most manifest?

III. *The importance of getting wisdom.* "How much better is it to get wisdom than gold!" Notice the words "to get," that is, to secure. Nor will it be obtained without earnest effort. Prov. ii. 3–5; Luke xiii. 24. The importance of getting wisdom is seen—

1. *In its great value.* If wisdom is worth so much, how needful to secure it! It is not needful for you to amass gold, or to encircle your brow with the laurel of fame; but it is a matter of infinite moment that you obtain the wisdom without which there is no salvation. This is the great attainment, in the absence of which all other attainments are worthless.

2. *Without it all is lost.* Man's true dignity as a rational

creature is lost. He desecrates his dignity if he gets not this wisdom. He loses his soul. Matt. xvi. 26. We see the greatness of this loss in the fact that the gaining of the whole world cannot be a compensation for it. This loss includes the loss of the divine favor, the loss of heaven, loss of a blissful immortality. Surely then I may say that, without the wisdom of the text, all is lost.

REMARKS.

I. The text reverses the common verdict, the world's verdict.

II. Fix not your hearts on gold.

III. Rightly appreciate, and earnestly seek wisdom.

UNSELFISHNESS.

We then that are strong ought to bear the infirmities of the weak, and not to please ourselves. Let every one of us please his neighbor for his good to edification. For even Christ pleased not himself.—Rom. xv. 1-3.

We know what selfishness is. It is undue self-love, which prompts the seeking of one's own interests at the expense and to the injury of the interests of others. It conflicts directly with what has been styled the Golden Rule, as given by Christ, in Matt. vii. 12: "All things whatsoever ye would that men should do to you, do ye even so to them." As selfishness is wrong, its opposite is right; and its opposite is unselfishness. This word, however, I do not find in my dictionaries, but as I have need for it I will use it.

UNSELFISHNESS.

My plan requires me to notice—

I. *How it manifests itself.* The text suggests that it does this in three ways, as follows:

1. *In bearing the infirmities of the weak.* What are the special infirmities referred to here, we may learn from

Romans xiv. 2, 3, 5, 14, 15, 19, 20, 21, 22, 23. Some of the members of the church at Rome objected, it seems, to eating flesh at all, and others, perhaps, only to eating the flesh that had been offered in sacrifice to idols. They were weak brethren, and Paul makes a courteous concession to their weakness, or, if you prefer the word, their prejudices. These are the infirmities referred to in the text. They are not to be found among us; but other infirmities can be found. How many weaknesses there are! The example of "the strong" may lead "the weak" into sin. We see from 1 Cor. viii. 8–11, how this can be. The example of the strong may grieve the weak. The strong may be able to do, without sinning, what the weak feel that they dare not do. Now in all such cases, the strong should bear the infirmities of the weak, by abstaining from that which would either lead the weak into sin, or wound their feelings. They should bear, too, the infirmities of the weak by hearty sympathy with them in their trials. There is wonderful power in Christian sympathy in lightening, and even in removing burdens of sorrow.

2. *In not pleasing ourselves.* Selfishness makes us please ourselves to the injury of others. Self-love permits us to please ourselves while we please others. The spirit recommended in the text arrests the operation of self-love so that there is no effort to please one's self, but a desire to please others. "Not to please ourselves." It is implied in these words that bearing "the infirmities of the weak" is not pleasant. It is not. You that are strong would find it more agreeable to have nothing to do with the infirmities of the weak. It would be easy to ignore them; and here, it may be, is your temptation, to let the weak alone. But what says the text? "And not to please ourselves." Consulting your own pleasure is the very thing you are not to do.

3. *In pleasing others for their good.* Pleasing others is the

opposite of pleasing ourselves. As we are not to please ourselves, we are to please others. It requires piety of an exalted type to make the two things coincide. It will be observed that there is a wise limit imposed on our pleasing others. We are not to try to please them in every way, and in every thing. The text says, "for his good to edification." Your object must be to promote the good of your neighbor by edifying him. To edify is to build up. The Christian character needs to be built up, strengthened, developed, put into symmetrical form. A wide field of labor opens here. The best way to please others for their good is to be forgetful of ourselves.

II. *The model of unselfishness.* "For even Christ pleased not himself." Here we have Paul's exhaustive and final appeal. We may suppose him to have thought within himself that some of the brethren would say, "This is hard, not to please ourselves." The apostle only says, "Christ pleased not himself." This does not mean that Christ engaged reluctantly in the work of redemption. There was no reluctance. The language brings out the great principle of self-sacrificing love. Christ did not please himself in the sense of consulting his own personal ease. To show this, let us consider—

1. *His incarnation.* Think you that, as the Eternal Word, he consulted his ease or his dignity in taking a finite nature into union with his divine nature? This finite nature, too, was resting under dishonor and ignominy, because of sin. What an act of condescension on the part of the Word to become flesh, to become man! Was there ease or comfort in the act?

2. *His poverty.* What read we in 2 Cor. viii. 9? Became poor! His birth introduced him to scenes of poverty with with which he continued familiar till his death. Look at his manger-cradle. Did he consult what you would call ease or pleasure in being born thus, and having "not where to lay his head"?

3. *His patience with his disciples.* They were very unpromising scholars, slow to learn. Did he consult his ease or pleasure in bearing with them?

4. *The opposition of his enemies.* "Consider him that endured such contradiction of sinners against himself." Calumny hurled at him its darts till its quiver was exhausted.

4. *His death on the cross.* What a death! Did he consult his ease?

REMARKS.

I. Ask yourself honestly and earnestly, Am I unselfish?

II. The example of Christ should become more and more influential.

SELF-FLATTERY.

All the ways of a man are clean in his own eyes.—Proverbs xvi. 2.

It is very often the case that men judge themselves and others by different standards. To others they apply rigid rules, and on themselves they pronounce merciful judgments. Sometimes they condemn in others what they excuse in themselves. In short, they are guilty of what I shall make my topic of discourse on this occasion, namely:

SELF-FLATTERY.

Of this great evil it may be said—

I. *It is a universal sin.* We all know what flattery is. It is undue, exaggerated praise. Simple praise—that is, praise within the limits of truth—is right, for it is only commendation of that which deserves to be commended. Flattery always goes beyond the bounds of truth. It is extravagant praise, prompted often by blind partiality, and too often by artful design. When we flatter others, if they believe us, they are led to think too highly of themselves. Now prefix *self* to flattery, and it becomes self-flattery. In this case a man thinks too highly of himself or of his ways. It is not wrong for persons to think of themselves in accordance with fact and truth. Rom. xii. 3. But when they form an inordinate estimate of themselves, of their character, talents, position, acts, or influence, they are guilty of the sin and folly of self-flattery. Especially do men engage in the work of self-flattery when they think it necessary to make excuses for their sins. Their minds are fruitful in the invention of these excuses. They reason so plausibly in justification of themselves that their ways are clean in their own eyes. "All the ways of a man are clean in his own eyes." Self-flattery covers up the marks of iniquity. It possesses the strange power of self-deception; for in self-flattery the agent and the object are one and the same. Self-delusion is therefore inevitable.

II. *Selfishness is the source of this sin.* When Paul says that in the last days men shall be lovers of themselves, he refers, no doubt, to what we mean by selfishness. But he did not refer to selfishness as having its origin in the last days; its operation is only to be intensified. Self-love, properly so called, is right. "Thou shalt love thy neighbor as thyself," justifies it. Selfishness is always wrong. It is self-love degenerated and perverted. It expunges the words "thy neighbor" from the Second Commandment, while it emphasizes and illuminates the word "thyself." Thou shalt love thyself is the language of selfishness. It is because men love themselves, so decidedly prefer themselves to others, that they indulge in self-flattery. They think they are better than others. If their ways are not clean, to refer to the text, their self-partiality supplies a deceptive medium through which they appear clean. Or, if they are not entirely clean, too often does the heart flatter itself into a belief that its motives are good—so good as to compensate for any thing wrong in the ways to which they lead. How true is it that men flatter themselves because of their selfish love! How contemptible is selfishness! How absurd to make *self* the center and circle of one's being and action!

III. *Consequences of self-flattery.* These consequences have to do with saints and sinners. With regard to the former, it may be said—

1. *Self-flattery obstructs Christian progress.* Christians should ever be in a state of progressive improvement. This we are taught literally in 2 Peter i. 5–7, and figuratively in 1 Cor. iii. 1; Heb. v. 12–14; 1 Peter ii. 2. Let a Christian through self-flattery persuade himself that he has made attainments which he has not made, and you can easily see how all spiritual progress is obstructed.

2. *It is an insuperable barrier to a sinner's repentance.* Let a sinner indulge self-flattery, and if he does not conclude that he is not a sinner at all, he reasons himself into the belief that his sins are trivial, and therefore excusable. Entertaining this view he cannot repent. The constitution of the human mind forbids. The case of the Pharisee (Luke xviii. 11, 12) illustrates this point. Was it possible for him to repent without a change of views concerning himself? Most manifestly not.

IV. *The remedy for self-flattery.* We should be glad that there is a cure for an evil so common and so great. We may find the remedy in the following considerations:

1. *God sees us as we are.* Men may flatter us and make us believe that we are greatly better than we are. We may flatter ourselves; our deceitful hearts may so deceive us as to make us think that wrong is right, and evil good; but God is not deceived. Self-flattery may weave in the loom of selfishness a covering, to be thrown as a disguise over the character; but what are disguises with God? One glance of his eye pierces through them and they vanish before him. He sees every man as he is, and looks at every heart as it is. 1 Sam.

xvi. 7; 1 Chron. xxviii. 9; Psalm cxxxix. What folly there is in self-flattery in view of the omniscience of God!

2. *Our opinion of ourselves does not influence the judgment of God.* He takes into account character and the substratum of character; what a man is, and what has made him what he is. Our opinions will have nothing to do with God's decisions. His judgment will sweep away all the sophistries of self-flattery.

3. *God's decision will be infallible and irreversible.* It will come into direct conflict with all the forms of self-flattery. Human decisions are fallible; God's are not. The decisions of earthly courts are reversible; but when God pronounces judgment, his sentence will be final, and therefore irreversible. From it there will be no appeal. How insane is self-flattery!

REMARKS.

I. Have you been guilty of the sin of self-flattery?
II. Guard against it diligently in time to come.
III. Think often of the unbiased judgment of God.

UNCERTAIN RICHES AND TRUE RICHES.

. . . Nor trust in uncertain riches.—1 Tim. vi. 17.

Who will commit to your trust the true riches?—Luke xvi. 11.

There are very few persons who do not wish to be rich. The desire of wealth is as universal as any desire except that of happiness. The general opinion, too, is that happiness can be secured by means of wealth. It is to be regretted that the term riches is applied almost exclusively to worldly possessions. Men forget that there are spiritual and eternal riches. They forget that there are the two kinds of riches named in my double text, which supplies this theme:

UNCERTAIN RICHES AND TRUE RICHES.

If we can comprehend this theme, we shall be profited by the services of this hour.

I. *Uncertain riches.* There is the greatest uncertainty connected with worldly riches. *Uncertainty of riches* is the literal rendering of the Greek. That riches are uncertain appears from two considerations:

1. *They are deceptive and unsatisfying.* They are supposed to be capable of meeting and gratifying the desires of the soul. Here comes in the deception. The supposition has often been indulged, but never realized. No amount of wealth has ever satisfied the cravings of the mind. In proof of this I refer to Eccles. ii. 4–11. Who will ever make a more thorough experiment than Solomon? But he was compelled to say: "Vanity of vanities. All is vanity."

2. *They are not permanent.* This fact emphasizes their uncertainty. If they were satisfying while they last, still they last but a little while. Uncertain riches! The transition from wealth to poverty, so far from being impossible, is very often exemplified. There are many persons once rich now poor. "The wheel of fortune," as it is called, makes many capricious revolutions. I think the estimate is that wealth does not continue in families more than two or three generations. There are, of course, some exceptions. There is no absolute security for any species of property. Floods may destroy it, tornadoes sweep it away, or flames consume it. Investments most carefully made may become worthless. Titles to the best real estate may prove to be defective. You dare not apply the epithet *certain* to any worldly possession, for the tenure by which you hold it is very precarious. All that I have been saying has reference to riches while persons live. We have seen the uncertainty of riches during life. But suppose them certain while life lasts: What then?

Life does not last. Death comes apace. Riches must be left when poor mortals are hurried into eternity. "For we brought nothing into this world, and it is certain we can carry nothing out." Here is something certain—"we can carry nothing out." Large accumulations may be made while we are in the world, but they cannot be carried out when we die. Truly there is no permanence in riches. They are in various ways taken from their possessors during life, or their possessors are taken from them at death. Uncertain riches.

II. *True riches.* Of these riches it may be said that those who possess them are truly rich. Their wealth is real, substantial. It is in striking contrast with the wealth of the world. The value of "the true riches" will be seen if we consider that they include such things as these:

1. *The saving favor of God.* Without this any man and every man is wretchedly poor. He may abound in what is called "worldly good," but he is a spiritual pauper. The words, saving favor of God, direct our attention to our lost condition as sinners. Being sinners, how greatly we need pardoning mercy! Without it we are undone. But it is included in God's saving favor. Those who receive this favor are freely pardoned; and not only pardoned, but justified, accepted in Christ, so that he becomes to them "the end of the law for righteousness." The robe of Christ's righteousness adorns them. It cost his obedience and blood to procure this robe. We estimate things by what they cost. How incalculable, then, the value of this robe of righteousness! Is it not included in "the true riches"? The saving favor of God is received by faith, and this reminds us of the import of the words "rich in faith." Those who have faith are rich, even as "the poor in spirit" are rich.

2. *A title to treasures in heaven.* What does Jesus say? "Lay up for yourselves treasures in heaven." Matt. vi. 20.

There are treasures, then, in heaven. What a safe place for them! How secure they must be! These treasures include all that is meant by the bliss and glory of heaven. They comprehend what Peter calls the "inheritance incorruptible, undefiled, and that fadeth not away, reserved in heaven." The title to this inheritance is as perfect as the oath and promise of God can make it. Those have the true riches, who have this title. All that is most sacred and precious in the blood of the everlasting covenant guarantees to them the title.

3. *Earnests of glory.* This point is to be distinguished from the foregoing one. Not only are there treasures in heaven, but there is an anticipation, a foretaste of them, which gives enjoyment now. These are earnests of glory. In law, "earnest money" ratifies a bargain, and is a pledge that the obligations of the contract will be met. Strictly speaking, an earnest differs from a pledge in this, that while the latter is not of necessity the same in kind with subsequent payments, the former always is. In referring, therefore, to earnests of glory, I mean that the spiritual life and love and joy which believers have on earth are the same in kind, not in degree, with the life and love and joy of heaven. These earnests are very precious, for they are prophetic and promissory of immortal glory. They are included in "the true riches."

REMARKS.

I. Place the proper estimate on "uncertain riches."

II. Set your hearts on the "true riches," and strive to gain them.

III. You may obtain them.

IV. If you do not, you will be miserable paupers to all eternity.

RESTORATION OF THE JOY OF SALVATION.

Restore unto me the joy of thy salvation.—Psalm li. 12.

When David uttered these words he was deeply and sorrowfully conscious of his departure from God. He knew that he had lost the experimental sense of God's gracious presence which he had often enjoyed. He had such a view of his polluted heart as made him feel his need of a pure heart. Hence he prayed, "Create in me a clean heart." Having lost the joy of God's salvation he earnestly desired to recover it. He therefore poured forth his soul in the words of the text. The topic which these words furnish is—

RESTORATION OF THE JOY OF SALVATION.

What I have to say will be under the following divisions:

I. *There is a joy of salvation.* It is a joy pertaining to salvation. It is the joy of the saved, and it grows out of the fact that they are saved. They rejoice in the salvation which is of the Lord. There is surely enough in this salvation to inspire joy; for it beneficially affects the past, the present, and the future. Notice—

1. *The past.* What was the former condition of those now saved? They were enemies of God; but love has taken the place of enmity. They were condemned, but justification has superseded condemnation; and the thunders of the divine law are hushed into peaceful and eternal silence. Is there not joy in this?

2. *The present.* "Beloved, now are we the sons of God." *Now*—in the present state, amid the infirmities of the flesh, and the trials of life. Is there not joy in the consciousness of sonship with God? There is the assurance, too, that all things are working together for their good.

3. *The future.* "It doth not yet appear what we shall be." It does not appear what our spirits shall be in their disem-

bodied state. Nor do we know how glorious our resurrection-bodies will be. We can form but a feeble conception of what eternal life is as exemplified in the glorified personality of the saints. But we know that the future will all be blissful. Am I not justified in saying that salvation beneficially affects the past, the present, and the future of the saved? There is, then, a joy of salvation.

II. *The joy of salvation may be lost.* I do not say the salvation, but the joy. How is the loss of this joy incurred?

1. *By leaving our first love.* This was the case with the church of Ephesus. Rev. ii. 4. The Christian's first love is ardent, and in union with it is holy joy. The joy is coeval with the love. When the believer leaves his first love, he loses the joy of salvation.

2. *By neglecting the Bible.* This volume God has given us to teach us what to believe and what to do. They are truly wise who learn the lessons it teaches. The truth of God as contained in his word is the means of sanctification. Neglect of this truth leads to sin; it is sin; and sin creates distance and darkness between God and the soul. The joy of salvation is lost.

3. *By losing the spirit of prayer.* When Christians are in a spiritual frame of mind they love to pray. No place is like the throne of grace. There is delight in prayer, and the joy of salvation fills the soul. But when the spirit of prayer is lost, or the duty is performed in a formal manner, the joy of salvation is lost. It cannot be preserved without communion with God in prayer.

4. *By imbibing the spirit of the world.* How difficult to live in the world and not be injured spiritually by its influences! Christians cannot love the world supremely, but they may love it inordinately. This inordinate love withdraws the affections from divine things. The injunction, "Set your affection on things above," is forgotten, and the joy of salvation is lost.

III. *Restoration of the joy of salvation.* The loss of the joy of salvation is a great misfortune, and a great fault. It is highly important, therefore, that the joy be restored. It is important—

1. *For our own comfort.* How wretched are we without the joy of salvation! There is no real happiness for us. There is a vacuum which all below the skies is incompetent to fill.

2. *For our usefulness.* What can you do as a church-member, if you do not enjoy the salvation of God? You cannot perform aright the duties you owe your fellow-members, nor the duties you owe the impenitent.

3. *For the honor of religion.* Many persons think religion a gloomy, repulsive thing. If those who profess it are not happy, dishonor attaches to it. What will men of the world say? The joy of salvation is so precious that it clothes religion with a halo of glory, and presents it in its beauteous aspect.

4. *For the glory of God.* When his people serve him as if they thought it a hardship, he is dishonored. When they serve him with joy and gladness, he is glorified. For these and other reasons the restoration of the joy of salvation is important.

IV. *Means of restoring the joy of salvation.* What are they?

1. *Thorough self-examination.* Without this we cannot know what has caused the loss of the joy of salvation, nor can we know what to do.

2. *Confession of the sins which have caused the loss of the joy.* See 1 John i. 9; ii. 2, 3.

3. *Repentance on account of these sins.* God forgives only those who repent.

4. *Abandonment of the sins that are confessed and repented of.*

5. *Earnest prayer.* The text is a prayer, "Restore."

REMARKS.

I. Has the joy of salvation ever been yours?

II. It is your privilege to rejoice in the Lord evermore.

III. The joy of salvation on earth is a foretaste of the joy of heaven.

IV. Sinners know nothing of this joy, and never will, unless they repent.

THE HONOR OF BEING A CHRISTIAN.

Yet if any man suffer as a Christian, let him not be ashamed; but let him glorify God on this behalf.—1 Peter iv. 16.

The term Christian is used but three times in the Scriptures, namely: Acts xi. 26; xxvi. 28, and in the text. Let us inquire—

I. *What is it to be a Christian?* An important question. I give a four-fold answer. It is—

1. *To believe in Christ.*
2. *To love Christ.*
3. *To be like Christ.*
4. *To obey Christ.*

Let us consider—

II. *The honor of being a Christian.* This honor is seen in two forms of expression in the text:

1. *Let him not be ashamed.* The reference is to suffering as a Christian. The honor of being a Christian is so great that he who suffers for Christ's sake has nothing to be ashamed of.

2. *Let him glorify God on this behalf.* The expression we have been considering is negative—not be ashamed. Here we have something positive. "Glorify God on this behalf." If called to suffer for Jesus' sake, the Christian should bless and praise God. How great then the honor of being a Christian! Acts v. 41.

3. *The Christian has a title to heavenly glory.* This, though not taught in the text, is abundantly taught elsewhere. Surely then there is great honor in being a Christian.

QUERY.

Are you a Christian?

LOVE TO ENEMIES.

But I say unto you, Love your enemies.—Matt. v. 44.

Who says this? The Great Teacher, who spoke as never man spoke. Jesus reversed the teaching of the Scribes and Pharisees. They said, as in verse 43, quoting correctly from Moses, "Thou shalt love thy neighbor" (Lev. xix. 18), but without a particle of authority they added, "and hate thine enemy." They made this addition with Proverbs xxv. 21, before their eyes. The Old Testament enjoins the love of enemies, and the New Testament emphasizes the injunction. Fix your thoughts on—

LOVE TO ENEMIES.

An enemy is one who hates. Are there any persons who hate you? If so, they are your enemies. Are you to hate them in return? Human nature, in its fallen state, answers, "yes." Jesus says, "no, but love them." You say, "how difficult, if not impossible!" Nothing you can say changes the command. Here it is in all its unrepealed force: "Love your enemies." It is my purpose to assign some reasons why we should love our enemies. The love of benevolence, not the love of complacency, is referred to. Why should we love our enemies?

I. *God loves his enemies.* The world abounds with his enemies. The Bible describes fallen men as "haters of God." This is a severe indictment, but its truth is as obvious as its severity. These are God's creatures, but they do not love him. They live on his bounty, but they are alienated from him. Their breath is in his hands, but they are his enemies. In their enmity they pervert God-given faculties. Their hatred does not extinguish his love. Nor is his love a quiescent feeling, shut up in the recesses of his own bosom. It seeks and finds expression, verse 45. The sun shines on his enemies, and the rain falls on his foes. These favors are representative of providential blessings. The supreme proof of God's love to his enemies is to be seen in the gift of his Son. 1 John iv. 10. We should be as much like God as possible. "That ye may be the children of your Father"—that is, prove yourselves to be his children.

II. *Jesus loves his enemies.* Their enmity rendered necessary his incarnation and death, in order to their salvation. Sins involved in this enmity must be atoned for, and there must be provision for the substitution of love. Think what Jesus did. 1 Tim. i. 15. He died for our sins. 1 Cor. xv. 3. He died for us while we were yet sinners. Rom. v. 6, 8. See his love in his death for his enemies. It is only through his death that his foes become his friends. Col. i. 21, 22. Christ's love of enemies is seen in the fact that the first offer of the salvation procured by his death was made to Jerusalem sinners. Luke xxiv. 47. Jesus has left us an example. 1 Peter ii. 21. We may not be required to die for our enemies, as Jesus did, but it is our duty to love them.

III. *Your enemies are your fellow-creatures.* Distinctions among men are chiefly artificial. On the plane of creatureship they stand on a perfect equality. You are God's creatures, and so are your enemies. Acts xvii. 26. You may say that this is a reason why creatures should not be enemies. So it is, but it is also a reason why, if you have enemies, you should love them. They belong to the human race as well as yourselves. Their birth introduced them into a world of sorrow and suffering, and yours did the same thing for you.

Their troubles and yours are, in many respects, the same You and they are *fellow*-creatures; and if any of them hate you, it does not release you from obligation to love them.

IV. *Your enemies will soon be in the grave.* True, they may live longer than you; but if you survive them, will it not be very painful to stand in the presence of their silent graves and say, "Here lie those I did not love"? "These are the ashes, and this the dust of the men and the women who while they lived were hated by me." Would you save yourselves from reflections so bitter, so excruciating, see to it that you love your enemies, that you may never stand by the grave of any one to whom you have been hostile. The grave has its lessons which we should learn.

V. *Your enemies will soon be in eternity.* The stroke of death that sends the body to the grave sends the spirit into the eternal world. It may be that some who are your enemies are Christians. This may, perhaps, be possible through their mistakes and imperfections. If Christians, they will be in heaven ere long. Would it not be awful for you to hate any who are to shine amid the splendors of the celestial world? But if your enemies, as is most probable, are God's enemies, then they are in the broad way to ruin. If they die unchanged they will soon be in hell. They will know what Jesus meant by the worm that dies not and the fire that is not quenched. Can you, would you, hate the wretched creatures who are to be miserable to all eternity? Ought you not to love your enemies? Is there not force in the reasons I have presented?

REMARKS.

I. Love to enemies must show itself. Do you ask how? See the words that follow the text.

II. The duty is a very difficult one, but it can by the grace of God be performed.

III. Love to enemies is a strong proof of piety.

ACQUIESCENCE IN THE WILL OF GOD.

Nevertheless, not my will, but thine, be done.—Luke xxii. 42.

This is the language of the most illustrious sufferer that ever appeared in this world of suffering. I need not say it is the language of Christ. It was spoken in the Garden of Gethsemane, when his soul was overwhelmed with deadly anguish. The cup presented by his Father for him to drink was inconceivably bitter, so bitter as to call forth the agonizing prayer, "O my Father, if it be possible, let this cup pass from me." Matt. xxvi. 39. But there was unmurmuring submission to the divine will—"not my will, but thine, be done." These words suggest my present topic—

ACQUIESCENCE IN THE WILL OF GOD.

I prefer the term acquiescence to resignation, but it is needless to say why. My purpose is to dwell on some motives to Christian acquiescence in the divine will.

I. *God has the right to do as he pleases.* He is the only absolute Sovereign in the universe. In the exercise of his sovereign pleasure he created all things. Worlds, angels, and men exist because it is his will that they exist. In all the dispensations of his providence he executes his own will. None can stay his hand, and none can, without blasphemous impertinence, say, "What doest thou?" David said, "My times are in thy hand." This is as true of us as of David. The time of birth, childhood, youth, middle age, old age, joy, sorrow, sickness, health, prosperity, adversity, and death—all these times are in God's hand. Has he not the right to arrange all these times as he pleases? Who can dispute his right? If his right cannot be questioned, it is plainly our business to acquiesce in what he does. We should say from the heart, "The will of the Lord be done." Certainly every Christian should say, "Not my will, but thine be done." It is most reasonable that he repeat the words of his Lord.

II. *God always pleases to do right.* It is as unquestionable that he pleases to do right as that he has the right to do as he pleases. The Judge of all the earth will do right. The infinite righteousness of his character makes it morally impossible for him to do wrong. Whatever he does is regulated by infallible wisdom. There are no mistakes in the administration of his government. There are mysteries in many of his dealings with us, but they are mysteries to us, not to him. They are all plain to his omniscient view. They are parts of a plan which, when fully unfolded, will appear perfect in conception and perfect in execution. If God always pleases to do right, we should acquiesce in what he does. In what ought we to acquiesce if not in what is right? Surely not in what is wrong.

III. *God has in view the spiritual welfare of his people in all the afflictive dispensations of his providence.* "If need be," says Peter, "ye are in heaviness through manifold temptations." Who is to decide as to the "need be"? Certainly not we, but God; and we are expressly taught that he chastens us "for our profit, that we might be partakers of his holiness." Heb. xii. 10. It is written that God does not "afflict willingly, nor grieve the children of men." Lam. iii. 33. If this is true of "the children of men," it is surely true of his people. He afflicts them with a kind of paternal reluctance, and it is for their good. The Christian graces often shine most brightly in periods of adversity. Faith becomes stronger, love more ardent, hope more vigorous, zeal more earnest, humility deeper, and patience can have her perfect work only in times of trial. The evangelical tendency of afflictive providences is to weaken our earthly, and strengthen our heavenly, attachments. We are prone to think too highly of this world. Prosperity invests earthly things with a delusive lustre; but adversity lets us see them in their true light. Surely we should acquiesce in God's dealings with us, if he has our good in view. Not to do so, would imply a disregard of our own best interests.

IV. *Acquiescence in the will of God makes us like Christ.* When he came into the world he said: "Lo, I come to do thy will, O God." During his ministry he said: "My meat is to do the will of him that sent me." John iv. 34. What an example of acquiescence in the divine will we have in the narrative of his agony in the garden! His recoil from the bitter cup was only momentary; he took it, and drank it to the dregs:

> How bitter that cup no heart can conceive,
> Which he drank quite up that sinners might live;
> His way was much rougher and darker than mine:
> Did Christ, my Lord, suffer, and shall I repine?"

Would you not be like your Lord? Then renounce your own will, and acquiesce in the will of God. Let the acquiescence be devout, reverential, cheerful. When you pray for the cup of sorrow to pass from you, qualify the petition, as Jesus did.

REMARKS.

I. Acquiescence in the will of God glorifies his name.

II. It is difficult to learn thoroughly the lesson of acquiescence; but with divine help we can learn it.

III. True happiness is found in perfect acquiescence.

IV. In heaven, we shall see that God did right in the darkest providence.

THE WEEPING SOWER A JOYFUL REAPER.

He that goeth forth and weepeth, bearing precious seed, shall doubtless come again with rejoicing, bringing his sheaves with him.—Psalm cxxvi. 6.

Unpromising enterprises, having their origin in difficulties and tears, sometimes result so favorably as to call forth rejoicing. Thus is fulfilled the Scriptural declaration, "Weeping may endure for a night, but joy cometh in the morning.' It is well that joy succeeds sorrow, and that smiles follow tears. It encourages the sad and revives the despondent. If in worldly undertakings gloomy beginnings sometimes turn out to be happy successes, what is to be said of spiritual enterprises? There is surely much more certainty in regard to the latter. Of these it may be said, "They that sow in tears shall reap in joy." The same truth is presented in the text. From it I deduce this topic—

THE WEEPING SOWER A JOYFUL REAPER.

You can imagine a literal sower in an Eastern country with sadness in his heart and tears in his eyes. But our business now is to consider the spiritual sower. What seed does he sow? Jesus answers in the parable of the sower: "The seed is the word." It is the truth of God. This seed is to be sown in the *soil* of the intellect and in the *subsoil* of the heart. It goes through the former to reach the latter. The gospel covenant has to do with the *mind* and *heart*. Heb. viii. 10. I name spiritual sowers as follows:

I. *Christian parents.* It is their business to sow the seed of the word of God. The minds and hearts of their children may present an unpromising field, the contemplation of which calls forth tears. Literal seed before it germinates must be moistened by water or its equivalent. Spiritual seed is best moistened by tears. Let Christian parents remember this; and while in their labors for the conversion of their children they are weeping sowers, they will, with the blessing of God on their efforts, become joyful reapers.

II. *Sunday-school teachers.* They are often discouraged. They fear they are doing no good. Some in their classes are inattentive. They almost despair. They look with tearful eyes to see if a single ray of light dawns on the darkness. Let such teachers sow the seed of divine truth even though their tears fall fast while they sow, and after a while they will be joyful reapers, bringing their sheaves with them.

III. *Ministers of the gospel.* They are most prominent among spiritual sowers. The command to them is, "Preach the word." On many kinds of soil they cast the seed. Discouraging indications sadden their hearts. Having delivered their message, they often ask the stereotyped question transmitted from Isaiah's day to the present time: "Who hath believed our report?" Let them sow in *tears.* Weeping ministers are one of the great wants of this generation. They would soon become joyful reapers of rich harvests.

IV. *Christians in general.* There is something for you all to do. You may not be Christian parents, nor Sunday-school teachers, nor ministers of the gospel, but you sustain other relations to your fellow-creatures. Other fields are before you; and in them you can sow the good seed of the word. Opportunity to sow this seed creates obligation to sow it. "Sow beside all waters." "In the morning sow thy seed, and in the evening withhold not thine hand." Sow, sow the seed, even if it is done with many tears, and in due time you will be transformed from weeping sowers into joyful reapers.

REMARKS.

I. Labor in the work of the Lord is not in vain.

II. This cannot be said of any other kind of labor.

SUPREME LOVE TO CHRIST.

He that loveth father or mother more than me, is not worthy of me; and he that loveth son or daughter more than me, is not worthy of me. —Matt. x. 37.

This text emphasizes the importance of

SUPREME LOVE TO CHRIST.

We must not only love him, but love him supremely. Why?

I. *Because of the supreme excellence of his character.* His claim to supreme love would not be valid in the absence of this excellence. The supreme excellence of Christ's character grows out of the fact that divinity and humanity are united in his person. I do not refer to divinity in a figurative or poetical sense, but as a high, sublime reality. I refer also to sinless humanity. What a character is Christ's! All that is glorious in supreme divinity, and every thing lovely in perfect humanity, may be found in this character. Surely Christ deserves our supreme love.

II. *Because he has loved us and died for us.* These two factors—his love and his death—intensify his claim to our love, originating in the transcendent worthiness of his character. Contemplate the strength of his love in view of what had to be done to gratify its impulses. He must lay aside his glory and become a man, a man of sorrows. Christ's love led him to die for us, and in his death we have the highest proof of his love, proof that can never be invalidated. Does he who has loved us and died for us, deserve our supreme love?

III. *Because supreme love to Christ is the essence of piety.* When we think of the prominent place which the gospel assigns to Christ, we may well tremble for those who reject his claims. Supreme love to Christ is the essence of piety in such a sense that he who does not love him is the enemy of all righteousness, and goodness, and truth. He is the enemy of God, and no heart can be right in the sight of God if destitute of love to Christ. No pure motive influences such a heart. Want of love to Christ so involves the absence of all that is right and good, that it is written, "If any man love not the Lord Jesus Christ, let him be Anathema Maranatha." 1 Cor. xvi. 22. In the view of piety now presented, we clearly see why we should love Christ.

PROOFS OF SUPREME LOVE TO CHRIST.

I mention a few, such as the following:

I. *A supreme appreciation of fellowship with him.* This fellowship is a blessed reality. John xiv. 21–23; 1 Cor. i. 9; 1 John i. 3. This fellowship with Christ is put far above all earthly joys by those who love him supremely; and when it is disturbed or lost, nothing can fill the sad vacuum in the soul. Then there is a verification of the familiar lines:

> But now I find an aching void
> The world can never fill.

II. *A supreme purpose of soul to do what Christ requires.* It is assumed by Christ that this purpose exists in all his disciples. Matt. xxviii. 20. He makes the doing of what he commands the test of love to him. John xiv. 21; 1 John v. 3. How can there be supreme love to Christ without this supreme purpose to do his will, and live to his glory?

III. *A supreme solicitude that others may love him.* It cannot be otherwise. The greater your love to Christ, the greater will be your anxiety for your fellow-creatures to love him.

REMARKS.

I. Do you love Christ with supreme affection?

II. Those who thus love him on earth will see his face in heaven.

TALENT-HIDING.

And I was afraid, and went and hid thy talent in the earth: lo, there thou hast that is thine.—Matt. xxv. 25.

This language is a part of what is commonly called the "Parable of the Talents." Important spiritual truths are in this parable, illustrated by reference to a man preparing to travel into a distant country. Calling to him three servants, he delivered to them his goods. To one he gave five talents, to another two, and to the third one. In due time he required these servants to render an account. What the first and the second said is recorded in verses 20–23. The text is a part of what the third said: "I was afraid, and went and hid thy talent in the earth." The topic of discussion is—

TALENT-HIDING.

I solicit attention to these points—

I. *God gives a talent to every one.* To some he gives a plurality of talents, but to every rational being not less than one. A general definition of this talent is the capacity of doing something for man's good and God's glory. Who is there that has not this capacity? It is optional with God to give it; but when it is given, its use is imperatively required. God has the right to require it. In other words, his creatures are under obligation to do what he commands. Their accountability grows out of their relation to him. It is therefore inseparable from their being. God gives, and requires an improvement of what he gives. It is vain to dispute the propriety of this; as vain as to deny the shining of the sun at noon-day.

II. *Talent-hiding is a common sin.* The example of the slothful servant is copied everywhere. "I hid thy talent"—that is, made no use of it, and therefore no improvement of it. I cannot name all the talents that are hidden or not used, but I will mention the following:

1. *The capacity to love God.* You cannot call in question the existence of this capacity without denying that man possesses the faculty of love. This you cannot deny. The faculty is in constant exercise, and has been in all ages. Men love the world, its riches, its honors, its pleasures. They love sin. They love one another and they love themselves. They therefore can love, but they do not love God. This is because the faculty of love is not rightly exercised, What did Jesus say? Mark xii. 30; John v. 42. What says Paul? 1 Cor. xvi. 22. How many in this assembly have, all their

lives, hidden the talent of which I speak! Their capacity to love God has not been exercised. The talent has been hidden.

2. *Influence.* This is a very valuable talent. It is a great power for doing good. If you had no influence, what good could you do? But you have influence. You exert it every day. It is felt wherever you go, and whatever you do. Many of you, however, are not exerting it for good, in your families, and in your daily associations. Your influence is against what is right and good. The talent is not used as its Giver requires. This is true of many professed Christians among us. Their light, if they have any, is under a bushel. They are hiding their talent of influence, or they are using it injuriously. Alas for them and for the cause of God!

3. *Property.* God gives this talent. Deut. viii. 17, 18; Acts xiv. 17. What we are to do with the talent of property we may learn very easily. Luke xvi. 9; 1 Cor. xvi. 1, 2. All that is said in the Bible in condemnation of the sin of covetousness is a rebuke of the sin of hiding the talent of property. The rich and the poor, and those midway between them, should give as they can. Giving is a part of worship. How grievously is this talent of property hidden in all denominations of Christians!

4. *Every opportunity for usefulness.* Do you see no opportunities of doing good? You would see a great many if your hearts were full of love and zeal. Are there no widows and fatherless ones to help? Are there no backsliders to be admonished? Are there no impenitent sinners to be talked with about their souls? Opportunities of usefulness are abundant, are all around you. You can do great good by kindly reproving your brethren and sisters who stay away from the house of God, or visit it very seldom. Every opportunity of usefulness that is not improved is a talent hidden.

III. *Excuses for talent-hiding are vain.* There can be no valid excuse. This will be seen if we consider—

1. *The talent is in possession.* The servant was not required to improve that which he had not. He had the talent, and it was as much trouble to bury it in the earth as to put it into the hands of the exchangers. So you have a talent. God has given it to you to be used for his glory; and to fail to use it is a great sin, for which there is no excuse. It is a criminal disregard of the will of God.

2. *That it is one talent is no excuse.* Many make this excuse, and it really condemns them. If they had many talents they might more plausibly try to justify the hiding of some, but their having one talent only is the very reason why it should be improved and not hidden. It is this or nothing. Something in the way of improvement must be done with the one talent, for there is nothing else with which to do anything. Surely the possession of one talent only is no excuse for hiding it.

3. *The slothful servant's excuse was vain.* Consider it. He complained of his lord, and even charged him with a disregard of every principle of justice, in reaping where he had not sown, and gathering where he had not strewed. His lord judged him out of his own mouth, virtually saying, If this was your opinion of me, that I was accustomed to take what was not my own, then you must have known that I would demand my own and the improvement of it. How absurd was the servant's excuse!

IV. *Talent-hiding is a dangerous thing.*

It must be so, for—

1. *It is rebellion against God.* It is an attempt to thwart his creative purpose. Why did he endow you as he has done? Was it not that you might glorify him? But in hiding your talent or talents you are acting in conflict with his purpose in your creation, and you disobey his will as expressed in his words.

2. *It makes life useless and worthless.* Whatever else a man

may do, if he hides the talent God has given him, he lives to no good purpose. What a thought is this! Life spent in an aimless way and therefore a blank! How it should startle us to think of a useless and worthless life!

3. *It shuts out of heaven.* "Cast ye the unprofitable servant into outer darkness." (Verse 30.) Heaven is a realm of light into which the unfaithful, talent-hiding servant enters not. "Outer darkness" is his place, and there "will be weeping and gnashing of teeth." Surely talent-hiding is a dangerous thing.

REMARKS.

I. Have you been hiding your one talent?

II. Bring it out from its concealment and begin this day to improve it.

PRAYING AMISS.

Ye ask, and receive not, because ye ask amiss.—James iv. 3.

Many persons do not pray at all. They live from day to day without thanking God for the favors he confers, or asking him for the blessings they need. They "restrain prayer before God." This is one of the ways in which wicked men were described in the days of Job. There are other persons who pray, pray regularly as the day comes; but they receive nothing in answer to their prayers. The reason is given in the text: "Ye ask, and receive not, because ye ask amiss." Theme—

PRAYING AMISS.

When do we pray amiss? I answer—

I. *When we are not earnest in our prayers.* Earnestness in prayer grows out of the high estimate we place on the blessings for which we pray. There must be suitable appreciation of what we pray for. Jesus says, "What things soever ye desire when ye pray, believe that ye receive them, and ye shall have them." Mark xi. 24. What says Paul in Rom. x. 1? Moses was in earnest when he prayed for the Israelites. Exodus xxxii. 32. It is a sin to ask God, in an indifferent way, to do any thing. What right have we to invoke his attention to any matter that we are not anxiously concerned about? Want of earnestness renders many prayers worthless. We pray amiss if we are not in earnest.

II. *When influenced by unworthy motives.* See the words following the text. A man may pray for health or wealth, intending to use it improperly. He may pray for greater spiritual blessings, in order that he may have a *reputation* for piety. He may pray for a revival, because he wants it to be said that the church he belongs to is doing well. He may pray for the salvation of his children, and his prayers may be prompted entirely by natural affection. God's glory may be overlooked. How many prayers are never answered, because they are polluted by impure motives. Unless we have the glory of God supremely in view, we pray amiss.

III. *When unwilling to give up any sin.* One important object of prayer is the promotion of holiness. An old writer has well said, "Praying will make us quit sinning, or sinning will make us quit praying." David says, "If I regard iniquity in my heart, the Lord will not hear me." Psalm lxvi. 18. Sin is infinitely hateful to God. How then can he hear the prayers of those who are unwilling to give up their sins? It cannot be. Such praying is praying amiss.

IV. *When we indulge an unforgiving spirit.* In the form of prayer which Jesus has given, we have these words: "And forgive us our debts as we forgive our debtors." The use of the word "trespasses" in subsequent verses, shows that by debts are meant sins. "As we forgive" is changed in the Revised Version, very properly no doubt, to "as we have forgiven," the perfect for the present tense. Think of this: When you pray you must be able to say, "As we have forgiven those who trespassed against us, so do thou, O God, forgive us." Is this not reasonable? If you cannot forgive the little offences committed against you, how do you expect God to forgive the great offences you have committed against him? If you cannot come over mole-hills, how can you think that he will come over mountains? Perhaps far more frequently than we think, an unforgiving spirit makes our prayers unsuccessful. The words of Jesus should cause us to tremble. Matt. vi. 15. If we do not forgive, we cannot be forgiven; and if not forgiven, we cannot go to heaven. Unforgiving brother or sister, settle this matter with Christ.

V. *When we are not willing to do whatever may promote the objects for which we pray.* If you pray to be more holy, you must diligently use all the means in your power to promote your sanctification. If you pray for the conversion of sinners, you must labor for their conversion. If you pray for the success of missions, you must give, if able, to the missionary cause. If not, you pray amiss. Sometimes, however, we can pray when we can do nothing else; as, for example, when our friends are at sea.

VI. *When we pray in an unbelieving spirit.* God has graciously made himself known as the hearer of prayer. If we pray, not expecting to be heard, we question his veracity. This is a great sin. It is a refusal to accord to God one of his attributes. Jesus established an important principle when he said to the two blind men, "According to your faith be it unto you." Matt. ix. 29. He wanted from them a recognition of his ability to do what they prayed him to do. We need not ask why God has made faith in his word essential to prevailing prayer. We know that such is the fact. Want of faith makes many a prayer worthless.

VII. *When our prayers are not presented in the name of Christ.* Jews do not use his name; nor do Deists, if indeed they pray at all. The name of Christ is studiously excluded from the prescribed forms of prayer in many of the Orders and Organizations among us. This is great folly, to attempt to approach God independently of Christ. John xiv. 6. But to present our prayers in Christ's name, is much more than the formal use of his name. It is to recognize him as Mediator between God and us, relying wholly on his mediation for acceptance at the throne of grace, and believing that no prayer will be, or can be answered, except for Jesus' sake.

REMARKS.

I. Do we not often pray amiss?

II. Let us correct our mistakes.

REJOICING IN GOD IN CALAMITY.

Although the fig-tree shall not blossom, neither shall fruit be in the vines; the labour of the olive shall fail, and the fields shall yield no meat; the flock shall be cut off from the fold, and there shall be no herd in the stalls: Yet will I rejoice in the Lord, I will joy in the God of my salvation.—Hab. iii. 17, 18.

There is in the prophecy of Habakkuk a reference to the invasion of Judea by the Chaldeans. They were to march through the land, and render it desolate. God was to permit it. Chapter i. 6. He is represented as doing what he suffers to be done. The Jews were to be punished for their sins, and the Chaldeans were to inflict the punishment. The prophet seems to have been overwhelmed with trouble and fear; he saw his country a desolation; but he soon recovered from his consternation by remembering that he had a source of joy which no calamities could reach. That source is indicated in the text. My topic is—

REJOICING IN GOD IN CALAMITY.

It will be well to consider—

I. *The calamity referred to.* Perhaps I should say the calamities, for there is a series of them; and taken together they make up the colossal calamity depicted by the prophet. Let us notice the several parts of this calamity.

1. *The fig-tree shall not blossom.* Figs constituted an important article of food with the Jews. Jesus sought fruit on a fig-tree. One tree, it is said, has been known to bear more than two hundred pounds of figs. The tree grows even in rocky places, where scarcely anything else will grow. The failure of the fig crop was a calamity.

2. *There shall be no fruit in the vines.* The grapes of Canaan were remarkable. The spies sent by Moses carried clusters so large that they were hung on a pole and carried by two men. It is said that even now a bunch of Palestine grapes often weighs twelve pounds. The vineyards are supposed to be unproductive—not to yield a scanty crop, but "no fruit." What a calamity!

3. *The labour of the olive shall fail.* The olive tree was the reliance of the Jews for oil, which they used for food, ointment, and light. It also produced wholesome fruit, about the size of a small plum. The tree lived about two hundred years. Its oil, mixed with wine, was good for bruises. Luke x. 34. For the labor of the olive to fail, was a serious matter.

4. *The fields shall yield no meat.* The products of the fields are referred to; chiefly the wheat and barley harvest. Meat does not mean flesh. A meat-offering under the Mosaic law, consisted of flour and oil. For the fields to yield no meat, was an utter failure of harvest. We can imagine what a calamity this would be to us.

5. *The flock cut off from the fold.* This refers to sheep and goats. These were very numerous among the Jews. Swine's flesh was prohibited as an article for food. This added to the value of sheep and goats, which were not only used for food, but in large numbers for sacrificial purposes. When the flock was cut off from the fold, prospects were gloomy.

6. *No herd in the stalls.* While sheep and goats were kept in folds, horses, mules, and cattle were kept in stalls. They were to be cut off. The stalls were to be empty. No animal to occupy a stall, and no food for it, if there had been. What a concurrence of calamities is supposed by the prophet! These calamities combined make a calamity of colossal magnitude, and worldly men of strongest nerve must sink under the paralysis of despair, appalling despair. But—

II. *The people of God may rejoice in him in calamity.* What says the prophet? "Yet will I rejoice." This little word *yet* is very emphatic:—yet, in spite of the calamity, I will rejoice in the Lord. There is no other source of real joy. All earthly joy depends on circumstances—this joy is above circumstances. Why may the people of God rejoice in him?

1. *Because their interest in him is not affected by calamities.* Let all the gloomy suppositions of the text be realized, still God himself is the portion of the soul. He may in his providence take all things from his people, but he never takes himself. Other things are to him as a drop to the ocean. Well does Cowper sing—

> Give what thou canst, without thee we are poor;
> And with thee rich, take what thou wilt away.

2. *God is the source of happiness.* He is called the blessed, or happy God. He is the God of all comfort. Happiness derived from him is transcendently superior to circumstances.

3. *He is the God of salvation.* "The God of my salvation," says the prophet. He is mighty to save, and loves to save. His saving mercy has found in the cross a way of egress from his benevolent heart. He gives the grace his people need.

4. *He makes calamities disciplinary and formative of complete Christian character.* They are among the "all things" which he makes "work together for good."

5. *He presides over death, and suffers it to do his people no real harm.* He takes away the sting of death.

6. *He finally receives his people to himself in heaven* There they will enjoy his beatific presence forever. In view of these precious truths may not every child of God, in the midst of calamity, say, "Yet will I rejoice in the Lord, I will joy in the God of my salvation"?

THE BLESSEDNESS OF THE PIOUS DEAD.

And I heard a voice from heaven saying unto me, Write, Blessed are the dead which die in the Lord from henceforth: Yea, saith the Spirit, that they may rest from their labors: and their works do follow them — Rev. xiv. 13.

It was well that John listened to a voice from heaven; for if he had hearkened to any of the voices of earth, he would have recorded something far different. He would have written, Blessed are the living, and specially those living in wealth, honor, and worldly splendor. The heavenly voice said, "Write," that is, commit to the imperishable pages of inspiration, for the comfort of the saints in all ages, the precious truth that the dead who die in the Lord are blessed. Theme—

THE BLESSEDNESS OF THE PIOUS DEAD.

You will observe that the blessedness is restricted to those who die in the Lord. This makes it proper to notice—

I. *What it is to be in the Lord.* The term Lord, in the New Testament, usually means Christ. This is its meaning here. To be in the Lord, then, is to be in Christ. We have the phrase in Christ in many passages of Scripture. Rom. viii. 1; 1 Cor. i. 30; 2 Cor. v. 17. In one place Paul refers to some who were in Christ before he was. To be in the Lord, in Christ, is to be in union with him. This union is symbolized by that between the vine and its branches, the body and its members, the foundation and its superstructure, the husband and the wife. All this imagery, striking as it is, is inadequate to express the intimacy of the union between Christ and his disciples. Hence the words, "*in the Lord*." We do not say, the patient is in the physician, or the client in the lawyer. There is no earthly union so close as to justify this form of expression; but the intimacy of the union between believers and Christ is indicated by the little word *in—in the Lord, in Christ.* This union is formed by faith, and can be formed in no other way. Faith is the sacred ligament that binds the soul to the Lord Jesus. Faith is a trustful reception of Christ; and when he is received the believer is in him—so in him as to be one with him. This union with Christ continues through all the scenes of mortal life. It is the province of death to break all other unions and sever all earthly relationships; but over the union between Christ and his followers death has no power. It is a death-defying union, which even gathers strength in the hour of dissolution, when all earthly alliances are broken like the spider's web. Hence the Christian dies in the Lord, sacredly and indissolubly united to him.

II. *The labors of those who are in the Lord.* They are said to rest from their labors, which implies that the labors continue till the period of rest comes. These labors include—

1. *Spiritual conflicts.* All Christians have these conflicts, for they grow out of the change which regeneration makes in taking the ascendency from "the flesh," or "the old man," and giving it to "the spirit," or "the new man." The flesh disapproves the change and the warfare begins and goes on while life lasts. It is the warfare to which Paul refers. Rom. vii. 14–25; Gal. v. 17. In the spiritual conflicts of the saints, "the old man," or "the flesh," is re-enforced by "this present evil world," and Satan avails himself of the world and the

flesh to carry into effect his malignant purposes. Truly there is labor in maintaining conflicts with enemies so formidable.

2. *Christian work.* "Always abounding in the work of the Lord," is the language of inspiration. The Lord has a work to be carried on in this world, and he is pleased to use his people for its accomplishment. It is a great honor to them to be employed by him. Paul refers to his fellow-workers (Col. iv. 11); and mentions the "beloved Persis, who labored much in the Lord." Rom. xvi. 12. The labors of the text embrace all the work that is done in the large circle of Christian activities.

3. *The endurance of trials and afflictions.* Paul said to himself, "bonds and afflictions abide me." In this age of liberty we are free from bonds; but affliction, in some of its diversified forms, comes upon all the people of God. They must "through much tribulation" enter into the heavenly kingdom. The redeemed before the throne of God came out of "great tribulation." We need not philosophize about the mystery of suffering; for we know that it is the will of God that his people, called by his grace, shall suffer for a while. 1 Peter v. 10. Their sufferings and trials are comprehended in the labors of the text.

III. *What the blessedness of the pious dead implies.* On this point I may say—

1. *Perfect deliverance from sin.* What is so distressing to Christians as sin? The devout Samuel Pearce explained the cause of his chief sorrow in these words: "The Being I love best always sees in me something which he infinitely hates." Sin is the great annoyance and burden of the people of God while they are in the body; but when they die the annoyance is gone, and the burden oppresses no more. Blessed are the dead who die in the Lord, for they are perfectly free from sin; are as holy as the angels of God.

2. *A cessation from the labors referred to.* All spiritual con-

flicts will be at an end, and peace without interruption will be enjoyed. As to work there will, doubtless, be the highest order of consecrated activity in heaven; but there will be no fatigue, no weariness. Here the saints, though not weary *of* the work of the Lord, are often weary *in* it. In heaven they will never become weary. All their sufferings will be over, while "sorrow and sighing shall flee away."

3. *A recognition of the works of the sainted dead.* "Their works follow with them." This is the Revised Version, and is doubtless correct. We can never protest too strongly against works of any kind as having to do with the matter of our justification before God; but the works which spring from faith and love are the testimonials of Christian character, and follow with the saints to glory. The pious dead will not be saved by works, but will be rewarded *for*, and "*according to* their works." Even the giving of a cup of cold water on earth to a disciple in the name of a disciple, will be followed by a reward in heaven. "Their works follow with them."

4. *The blissful presence of the Lord.* There is a cheerless theory that the spirits of the sainted dead become unconscious at the death of the body, and so remain till the resurrection. Paul teaches a very different doctrine. We learn from him, or rather from the Holy Spirit through him, that the spirit of the believer, while at home in the body, is absent from the Lord, and that when it leaves the body it is immediately present with the Lord. 2 Cor. v. 8. What words! Present with the Lord. There is an enjoyment of the exquisite bliss which the glorious presence of the Lord imparts. The saints on earth have the gracious presence of the Lord; in heaven they have his glorious presence. This is a part, and it seems to us, the chief part of their blessedness. "In thy presence," says David, "is fulness of joy."

5. *A glorious resurrection of the body.* This part of the blessedness of the pious dead is future, but not less certain on

that account. The saints will, doubtless, receive a large accession to their bliss at the resurrection. It is called "the adoption, to wit, the redemption of our body." Rom. viii. 23. It is not a re-creation, but a literal resurrection, that is, a rising again. "This corruption must put on incorruption." The same bodies that fall into the grave corruptible will be raised incorruptible, and fashioned like the glorified body of Jesus. They will be bright as the sun, and beauteous as heaven.

6. *Everlasting life in heaven.* The spirits of the sainted dead will, at the resurrection, be reunited to the bodies they formerly inhabited. Then will the redeemed, in their complete and glorified personality, enter upon the enjoyment of everlasting life. This life will not be merely everlasting being, but everlasting *well*-being. It will be disturbed by no apprehension of death. With all the accompaniments of heavenly glory it will be prolonged through endless ages, and made commensurate with the life of God. True, it is said of God that he "only hath immortality," but this means that he is the only Being who is inherently immortal. The saints derive their immortality from God, and, so far as the future is concerned, are as immortal as he.

REMARKS.

I. There is much to comfort us when the saints die. They are blessed in death and after death.

II. A vital question is, Are we in the Lord?

III. Woe to those who die, not in the Lord, but without Christ.

THE SAFETY OF YOUNG MEN.

Wherewithal shall a young man cleanse his way? by taking heed thereto according to thy word.—Psalm cxix. 9.

Young men are objects of great interest. No wise person can think of them without solicitude. Soon the places now filled by their fathers must be filled by them. They must be farmers, mechanics, manufacturers, merchants, lawyers, physicians, legislators, judges. In short, under God, the destinies of this country, and of all other countries, will soon be in the hands of those who are now young men. Bright or gloomy possibilities are before them. If they act well their part, the future is full of hope; if not, days of darkness will come. How then shall young men be prepared to meet their obligations? The text tells us, and it leads me to speak of—

THE SAFETY OF YOUNG MEN.

It may be said concerning them, that—

1. *Their way is amid the defilements of sin.* All the descendants of Adam are born under unfortunate disabilities. They inherit from him constitutional tendencies to evil. These tendencies are embraced in what is called "original sin." This sin shows itself in actual sin, when the period of accountability is reached. There are no exceptions in civilized or savage lands. There is actual sin everywhere. The world is full of sin. Every man, whatever he may think of himself, says that all other men are sinners. If what he says is true, they are sinners; if not, every man lies, and therefore all men are sinners. Sin is in the world, and the text implies that it is defiling. Hence the words, "cleanse his way." There is nothing so defiling as sin. It pollutes whatever it touches, and leaves its contaminating stain.

2. *Their danger is in contracting these defilements.* They have, as well as others, a depraved nature, and all exhibitions of depravity witnessed by them are perilous to character and conduct. Peter writes of the "pollutions of the world," and young men, more than others, are exposed to these pollutions. Their energy and enterprise impel them to go in all directions, and to illustrate all forms of activity. To avoid contact with the defilements of sin, is to young

men a very difficult thing. They are in danger from the skeptical philosophy of the age, from the influence of fashionable sins, from the coarseness of animal gratifications and licentious pleasures. If conscience condemns, there is at once a temptation to silence her voice, amid the clamor of appetite and passion. Truly, young men are in danger from the defilements of sin.

3. *Young men may cleanse their way.* The defilements of sin, though seen on every hand, may be avoided. There is no fatal necessity that they be contracted. Danger is not necessity. There is, however, but one method by which young men can cleanse their way. It is by giving attention to the word of God. This word tells what sin is. It reveals God as possessing all possible perfections, his holiness being the crowning glory of his character. It exhibits him as a Being who claims reverential homage, supreme love, and faithful service. The word of God is the only standard of right. The basis of right is to be found in the nature of God. His will is expressed in his word; but if we ask why he wills as he does, we have to say, because his nature is as it is; that is, because he is the Being he is. His character is perfect, and his will partakes of his character. It follows that his will, as expressed in his word, is the only standard of right. Adherence to this standard is the only way to avoid the pollutions of sin. Therefore, I say, emphatically—

4. *Young men, to cleanse their way, must accept the word of God.* Observe, they are to take heed to their way according to the word of God. Taking heed is all-important. It is the opposite of carelessness and listlessness. He who takes heed to his way is very anxious to know that his way is right, and this he can ascertain only by comparing it with the divine word. But why is the word of God the means by which young men may cleanse their way? I answer—

a. It teaches them what to believe. There can be no security for proper practice apart from correct belief. What men do depends on what they believe. Young men, to cleanse their way, must believe what the Bible says about God, about themselves as sinners, and about Christ as the Saviour.

b. It teaches them what to do. Having sinned, it is their duty to repent. They are required to do this, believe in Christ, make a baptismal profession of their faith, and consecrate their lives to the service of God.

c. It presents the most powerful motives to holiness. These motives are found in all the appeals that are made to the hopes and fears of men.

d. It points to examples worthy of imitation. We see these examples in such men as Abraham, Joseph, Samuel, Daniel, Paul, John, etc. It presents one perfect example—that of Christ.

e. It warns by bad examples, as seen in Cain, Pharaoh, Absalom, Judas, Ananias and Sapphira.

f. It teaches that prayer for divine help will be heard. All self-dependent effort will fail. Prayer brings help from heaven.

REMARKS.

I. Young men, is your way clean?

II. You see in view of this subject how to make it so.

III. Cleave with devout adherence to the word of God.

CHRIST KNOCKING AT THE DOOR.

Behold, I stand at the door and knock: If any man hear my voice, and open the door, I will come in to him, and will sup with him, and he with me."—Rev. iii. 20.

We all understand what is meant by knocking at a door. Our object in knocking is to gain admittance, and to gain it by consent of the occupant of the house. Cottagers knock at the doors of cottagers, and philosophers at the doors of philosophers. Seldom is the philosopher seen at the door of the hovel. It would be marvelous for kings to ask admittance into the habitations of their subjects. The knock of royalty at the cottage of poverty would be thought great condescension. But infinitely greater is the condescension to which the text directs our attention. The King of kings speaks; the Lord of glory utters his voice; let the universe listen: "Behold, I stand at the door and knock." The heart is represented as a mansion accessible by a door. At this door Jesus stands knocking. This is my topic of discourse—

CHRIST KNOCKING AT THE DOOR.

It will aid our thoughts to observe the following method:

I. *How Christ knocks at the door of the heart.*

On this point I remark—

1. *By his word.* The gospel is the word of Christ, and it tells of his salvation. Preachers are ministers of Christ. Sinners are subjects of gospel address. The Saviour speaks to them in his word, through his ministers, and asks them to open their hearts, that he may enter in. Christ stands at the door of the sinner's heart, as an humbled, crucified, risen, glorified, Saviour, and says: "Permit me to come in." He is an infinitely desirable guest. The heart has affections. It must love some object. Christ is supremely worthy of love. The Saviour makes an appeal to men's hopes and fears, desire of good, and fear of evil. Through these powerful springs of human action he knocks at the heart. He avails himself of the sinner's conscience.

2. *By his providences.* He is "Head over all things," and controls all events. By those providences which give prosperity he appeals to the gratitude of those at whose hearts he knocks. There are afflictive providences. Afflictions come not by chance. Has disease assailed you? Have you on a sick-bed seen the vanity of earthly things? Jesus has

knocked at the door of your heart. Have you lost the wealth and honor of the world? The Redeemer has said, "Receive me, and with me true riches and honor.' Have your friends been removed by death? Perhaps they occupied so large a space in your heart as to leave no room for Christ, and he has removed them to make a place for himself.

3. *By the Holy Spirit.* The Spirit reproves of sin. His agency is secured through Christ's mediation. He is the Spirit of Christ. Whenever, therefore, the Spirit operates on the heart, Christ may be considered as knocking for admittance. The Spirit glorifies Christ by fitting the heart for his temple. When the Spirit performs his work, Christ dwells in the soul as the hope of glory.

II. *The duty of sinners in view of Christ's knocking.*

The duty is threefold:

1. *They should reverently listen.* He utters his voice, as we have seen, in his word, in his providences, and by his Spirit. He says, "Unto you, O men, I call, and my voice is to the sons of man." Sinners must hear the call.

2. *They should repent bitterly that they have kept the Saviour out of their hearts so long.* It is better to say *you* than they. You have admitted other guests into your hearts, —earthly friends, the world, your lusts even. How wicked to keep your best friend out! How should your hearts be broken with sorrow! Do you not see the propriety of the gospel doctrine of repentance?

3. *They should at once open the door of the heart.* Christ will not make forcible entrance. The door must be opened voluntarily. The highest place in the affections must be assigned to the heavenly guest. All unworthy guests must be expelled. To open the door of the heart is to admit Christ; and to admit him is to love him.

III. *What follows the entrance of Christ into the heart.*

He enters as soon as the door is open. "I will sup with him, and he with me." This language intimates companionship and fellowship. There is communion between Christ and his disciples. The communion is the result of union, and the union is most intimate, finding its fullest definition in the words, "IN CHRIST." They are in him and he is in them. Friends sup at the same table, and this indicates equality. So the supping between Christ and those in whose hearts he figuratively dwells, expresses a blessed equality. "He that sanctifieth and they who are sanctified are all of one; for which cause he is not ashamed to call them brethren." "He is the first-born among many brethren."

REMARKS.

I. How much Christ desires our salvation!

II. How worthy is he of a place in our hearts!

III. Fellowship with him here is an earnest of the fellowship of heaven.

IV. Let sinners remember that Christ will not always knock.

THE EVIL OF SIN.

PART I.

. . . That sin by the commandment might become exceeding sinful. —Rom. vii. 13.

Sin is a short word, but it is one of tremendous import. Its history, including its nature, its turpitude, and its consequences, neither man nor angel could fully write. God alone can tell the universe what sin is in itself, and in its various bearings; and should he declare its malignity, as it appears to him, no finite mind could take in the awful idea. But, my friends, as we are sinners, it becomes us to acquaint ourselves as well as we can with the evil of sin. We should remember, too, that redemption through Christ presupposes that we have been ruined by sin. The words of the text are suggestive of this topic—

THE EVIL OF SIN.

There are many proofs of the evil of sin, some of which I present for your consideration.

I. *Sin is a violation of the creature's obligations to the Creator.* I assume it as a fact that all rational beings are under obligation to God. This obligation grows necessarily out of the relation they sustain to him. This being so, the continuance of the relation determines the duration of the obligation. If the relation is temporary, the obligation is temporary; but the relation is eternal, and therefore the obligation is eternal. While obligation arises from the relation referred to, it can be greatly strengthened. Every blessing conferred strengthens it. So far, then, as human beings are concerned, providence and redemption intensify obligation. We are now prepared to say that man's obligations to God are strong, sacred, imperative, and eternal. If so, is not sin a great evil? for it violates these obligations. It defies their strength, trifles with their sacredness, scorns their imperativeness, and disregards their eternity. I here personify sin, but I mean to convey the idea that the man who sins, does all this. He acts in direct opposition to the will of God. This will has been expressed in the divine law. Sin is so contrary to the precepts of the law, that by the law or commandment it "becomes exceeding sinful," as the text teaches. Sin is so bad a thing, that the strongest epithet defining it is derived from itself—*sinful.* It is "exceeding sinful."

II. *Sin is the voluntary act of rational beings.* An irrational creature cannot commit sin. Human governments do not hold idiots and lunatics responsible; because, in the case of the former, rational powers have never been developed; and in the case of the latter, though once developed, have been subsequently impaired. There is no basis of moral accountability. Sin implies the exercise of the moral powers, which can exist only in connection with a rational nature. Why are not brutes accountable? Because they are not rational. The possession of rationality, then, renders angels and men proper subjects of moral government. But while sin is the act of a rational being, the very fact that the being is rational should keep him from sinning, for he knows better. Rationality enables the creature to understand the obligations of which I have spoken. Do you not see that the evil of sin is great, because it is the act of a rational being? But I have said it is the *voluntary* act. There is no compulsion. Men never act more freely than when they sin. They follow their inclinations, and this is the essence of free agency. Now the voluntariness of sin adds to its turpitude. If it were the result of coercion, its demerit would be destroyed. There would be no demerit. Do you not see that sin is a great evil because it is the voluntary act of rational beings?

III. *Sin is committed in opposition to the most weighty considerations prompting to holiness.* Of these considerations I name the following:

1. *The glory of God.* Holiness glorifies him, sin dishonors him. The glory of God should be supremely dear to his creatures; but those who sin care not for that glory. So far from it, they are guilty of high treason against the Majesty of heaven.

2. *The avoidance of his wrath.* "The king's wrath is as the roaring of a lion," because a king, especially an Oriental king, has power to execute his wrath. How dreadful, then, must be the wrath of God! Sin excites it, and nothing else does. This wrath is righteous indignation against sin. Whatever makes it desirable to avoid the wrath of God is a motive to holiness.

3. *The desire of happiness.* This desire is deeply im-

planted in the soul, and holiness is indispensable to its gratification. Surely the desire for happiness is a strong motive to holiness.

4. *Self-interest.* Sin is man's worst enemy. He that sins against God wrongs his own soul. Prov. viii. 36. He disregards the appeal which self-interest makes in favor of holiness.

5. *Prospect of heaven.* The pure in heart, and those who follow holiness, shall see the Lord. Matt. v. 8; Heb. xii. 14. A course of sin is, in effect, a surrender of the hope and prospect of heaven. What weighty considerations prompting to holiness have now been presented! But sinners setting them all aside, transgress the divine law, and reject the salvation of the gospel. Is not sin an unspeakably great evil?

REMARKS.

I. How true is it that "Fools make a mock at sin"!

II. How should Christians tremble at the thought of committing sin!

III. How should they rejoice in hope of final deliverance from sin!

THE EVIL OF SIN.

PART II.

. . . That sin by the commandment might become exceeding sinful. Rom. vii. 13.

In continuing my proofs of the evil of sin, I present my fourth argument, as follows:

IV. *Sin is a great evil, because it required the obedience and death of Christ to atone for it.* We judge of a disease by the remedy resorted to for its removal. If a powerful remedy is applied, we infer that the disease is a dangerous one. What, then, shall we say of sin, expiable only by Christ's obedience and blood? The sacrifices of the law made *ceremonial* atonements, but there was no removal of *moral* guilt. In the latter sense they could not take away sin. The cattle on a thousand hills would have been offered in vain. "Silver and gold," by which multitudes have been ransomed from literal captivity, were uncurrent in the realm of redemption. The incarnation of an angel, or of the "innumerable company of angels," would not suffice. No, the Eternal Word must become incarnate. Bethlehem must witness his birth; Gethsemane must become vocal with his cries of anguish; and Calvary must be bathed in his blood. Sin is so great an evil that God the Father, the Lawgiver, could not connive at it when charged, not personally, but by imputation only, to his beloved Son. Then it was that Christ was "made a curse for us," was "made sin" in such a sense that "it pleased the Lord to bruise him," and "put him to grief." That sin could not pass with impunity, so as to supersede the necessity of the atoning death of the cross, is a fact which speaks with solemn significance to more worlds than this. This death was indispensable to the salvation of sinners, because sin is an evil which language has not power to define.

V. *The evil of sin may be argued from its consequences.* Contemplate Satan and fallen angels. Once they dwelt in light, but they sinned and were cast out of their bright abode into the realms of darkness. Consider our first parents in Eden. They were happy, but in an evil hour they ate the fruit—

> Of that forbidden tree, whose mortal taste
> Brought death into the world, and all our woe.

The earth was cursed for man's sake. Thorns and thistles burst spontaneously from its soil, and the decree went forth, that Adam and the toiling millions of his descendants should eat bread in the sweat of the face. All the sorrow that has crushed human hearts through the ages, has been the offspring of sin. All the tears that have flowed in every land and on every sea, have been the effects of sin. It was sin that called for the flood to submerge the guilty race of mortals. Death entered the world by sin, and has reigned from Adam to Moses, and from Moses till now. Some are dying at this moment. Sin has opened every grave, and requires "mother earth" to take her dead children to her cold bosom. Nor are the effects of sin confined to this world. There is a world of woe. There is an undying worm, and there is unquenchable fire. There is the second death, which is eternal death. All that the Bible means by the term *hell*, is the result of sin. Do you not see the evil of sin in view of its consequences?

REMARKS.

I. Sin, being so great an evil, it is infinitely reasonable that sinners repent. Every heart should be broken with sorrow on account of it.

II. Those who die in their sins will be lost forever. There is no exercise of pardoning mercy in the eternal world.

RELIGIOUS INDECISION.

How long halt ye between two opinions?—1 Kings xviii. 21.

Strange to say, the Israelites were hesitating whether to serve the God of their fathers, or to turn from him to the service of Baal, the idol god of the Syrians. Their minds seemed to have been in a state of culpable indecision, and the prophet Elijah said to them, "How long halt ye between two opinions?" I have selected this text because I am sure there are persons present who are thus halting. When they think of the value of their souls, and the importance of eternal things, they are almost persuaded to be Christians; but their love of sin and of the world prevents a full persuasion. How lamentable that accountable beings should be undecided on the subject of salvation! But so it is, and hence I select as the theme of discourse to-day—

RELIGIOUS INDECISION.

Please ponder —

I. *The unreasonableness of this indecision.*

Many unconverted persons are extravagant in their praises of reason. Some of them exalt it at the expense of revelation. Let us see, then, if religious indecision is not contrary to reason.

1. *It is reasonable for the creature to love the Creator.* There is nothing more reasonable than the first and great commandment of the law: "Thou shalt love the Lord thy God." But the subjects of religious indecision hesitate whether or not to give the affections of their hearts to God. Their indecision implies doubt as to the justice of God's claim to their love. Can any thing be more unreasonable than this?

2. *It is reasonable for perishing sinners to accept Christ as the Saviour.* Is it not reasonable for a drowning man to accept the assistance proffered to him in the hour of his extremity? Would not his rejection of it indicate insanity, the dethronement of reason? Those who are undecided in religious matters, hesitate as to an acceptance of the Lord Jesus. They know, too, that Christ is the only Saviour, and that there is no hope of salvation apart from him. The solemn alternative is, accept Christ and be saved, or reject him and be lost. How manifest the unreasonableness of not accepting Christ!

3. *It is reasonable to provide for the future.* The wisdom of the ant in laying up in summer stores for future use, is commended by Solomon. It is wise to provide for old age, so that its infirmities may be alleviated. But there is a future state of being. There is an eternity before us. There is a heaven and there is a hell. Is it not reasonable that we avoid the

latter and prepare for the former? Does not reason dictate that we provide for the future exigencies of our being? If so, religious indecision is most unreasonable, because it prevents all preparation for another world.

II. *The sinfulness of religious indecision.*

Why is it sinful?

1. *Because God prohibits it.* He requires decision. He says, "Choose you this day whom ye will serve." "Cease to do evil." Let the wicked forsake his way." "Strive to enter in at the strait gate." "Repent and be converted." In requiring decision and present action, God prohibits indecision and inaction. To be undecided, then, is to disobey God. Surely it needs no argument to prove the sinfulness of disobedience to God. There is always wickedness in refusing to do what God requires. His command is reason enough for doing the thing commanded.

2. *The undecided call in question the truth of what God says.* In his word he teaches us that salvation is all-important, the one thing needful; that the righteous only shall go to heaven; that the wicked must go to hell; and that the part we act in this short life will have a material, decisive bearing on our eternal destiny. The undecided do not believe, certainly do not fully believe, these things, or they would not remain undecided. They question the veracity of God. Is there not sin in this?

3. *The undecided exert an injurious influence.* In the circles in which they move they virtually say that religion does not demand decided attention. Thus they encourage others to neglect salvation, and they do this in violation of the command, "Thou shalt love thy neighbor." No man has a right to injure his fellow-men. There is sin in so doing.

III. *The danger of religious indecision.* In illustration of this point I present, but do not expand, the following thoughts:

1. *There is danger, because the longer sinners indulge this indecisive spirit the less probable their conversion becomes.* No one becomes a Christian while in a state of religious oscillation. There must be a thorough decision a full purpose to be the Lord's. But indecision may go so far as to preclude this purpose.

2. *There is danger, because God may leave the undecided to themselves.* Then they will decide indeed, but what a decision! to work out their own destruction by persistence in sin. "The wages of sin is death."

3. *There is danger, because the day of mercy is rapidly passing away.* "No bird has flight like time." No arrow speeds its course more rapidly. Let death come, and the sinner's character receives a stereotype impression, and his destiny is fixed. Is there not danger?

REMARKS.

I. Religion requires decision of character.
II. How unwise to halt between two opinions!
III. Many will deplore their indecision forever.

THE RESPONSIBILITY OF CHOICE.

Choose you this day whom ye will serve.—Joshua xxiv. 15.

These words were spoken amid circumstances of great solemnity. Joshua who, as successor of Moses, had superintended the settlement of the Israelites in the promised land, was about to die. He called for "all Israel" and through "the elders," "judges," and "officers" of the people, spoke to the twelve tribes. He gave a summary of patriarchal Israelitish history, or rather, he represents God as giving it. Verses 3–13. Joshua calls on all the people to fear and serve the Lord. Verse 14. "But if it seem evil to serve the Lord, choose you this day whom ye will serve." They are required to exercise choice, and this fact is suggestive of the subject we shall now consider—

THE RESPONSIBILITY OF CHOICE.

Observe—

I. *The command—"choose."* The power of choice is a great and blessed power. You will say this power is often abused. Yes; but still it is well that the power exists. That is, it is well that we are not machines, and that we are not controlled by an irresistible fate. Between the service of God and the service of sin, men are obliged to choose. The choice of one thing is the refusal of its opposite. To choose the service of sin is to refuse to serve God, and *vice versa.* You are all choosing and refusing now. You are responsible for the choice you make. You may question this. Many persons do. They know that choice is determined by the state of the heart, and they deny that they are responsible for the state of their hearts. This is the very thing they are responsible for. If not for this, they are responsible for nothing. Why is a man responsible when he commits murder? For no other reason than that he is responsible for the state of his heart. He is not responsible for taking life, killing, if it is accidental. Why? Because there is not such a state of heart as involves guilt. The "malice aforethought" is absent. Now if you are responsible for the state of your hearts, and if the state of the heart controls the choice, the responsibility of choice is thrown on you, and you cannot throw it off. You are required to choose life and not death, blessing and not cursing, the service of God and not the service of sin. I call on you to make the wise choice; to choose, like Mary, the good part. God offers himself to you as your portion. Will you not choose him? On the one side are offered to you the pleasures of sin, which are but for a season, to be followed by the bitterness of everlasting death; and on the other the service of God, with its sacred joys here, to be followed by eternal glory in heaven. Choose, choose whom ye will serve. You are responsible for the choice you make, and are obliged to choose. The text says, "choose"; God says, "choose."

II. *Who are to choose?* The text says, "*you.*" The "*you*" referred tc by Joshua were Israelites, for whom and for whose fathers God had done great things. He brought them out of Egypt, through the Red Sea and the wilderness, into a goodly land. What has he done for *you* to whom I speak? He has given you a home in the most desirable country on which the sun shines. He has blessed you abundantly. What an advantage, in living under the gospel economy, you have over the ancient Israelites! You have heard of Christ and salvation from your earliest years. When you were infants in your cradles the music of Zion's songs, sung by your mothers, soothed you to sleep, and the sound of salvation has been familiar to you to this day. Will you not choose God as your portion? Will you not choose Jesus as your Saviour? Will you not choose heaven as your eternal home? You are immortal creatures, but a little lower than the angels. You cannot maintain the dignity of your rational nature unless you choose to serve the God that made you. If you do not make this choice, you will act in a manner unworthy of your relation to eternity. Choose *you*, ye children in the bloom of youth, ye middle-aged in the vigor of your strength, ye old men and women, whose feeble steps show that you are tottering near the grave. I call upon you all to choose. The text says, "choose *you.*"

III. *When is the choice to be made?* The text says, "this day." We have similar language elsewhere. "To-day if ye will hear his voice, harden not your hearts." If the blessings of salvation are important, they should be sought without delay. The choice enjoined in the text should be made at once, for such reasons as these:

1. *It is by no means certain that it will ever be made, unless made this day.* The longer a sinner refuses to repent, the less probable his repentance becomes. Some cause produces the refusal, and that cause, it is most likely, will operate as powerfully in all future time as it does now. Sin is added to sin. The heart becomes harder. The improbability of the conversion of those unwilling to become Christians "this day" is very great. It is alarming.

2. *The soul is defrauded of the joy of salvation till the choice is made.* There is joy in the love and service of God. The joy bears date from the acceptance of Christ by faith. Rom. v. 1; 1 Peter i. 8. Choose salvation "this day," that your joy may begin.

3. *Making the choice to-day, you will become heirs of heaven.* Those who are God's children are his heirs, and joint heirs with Jesus Christ. What spiritual, everlasting riches will be yours; for you will inherit from your Father, who has at his disposal the resources of the universe.

4. *Not making the choice to-day, you may lose your souls.* What a calamity will that be! disastrous, ruinous, endless! What does Jesus say? Matt. xvi. 26.

REMARKS.

I. The solemn responsibility of choice rests on you.

II. What choice will you make?

III. Angels feel a benevolent interest in your decision.

MORAL INSANITY.

Madness is in their heart while they live.—Eccl. ix. 3.

When the mental faculties perform their appropriate offices, we say the mind is sane; but when these faculties become disordered in their action, we say the mind is insane. How pitiable are the subjects of mental insanity! They deserve the sympathy of the world. But there is an insanity so common as scarcely to attract attention. It is far more deplorable, too, than mental insanity. I refer to moral insanity. Multitudes of persons act insanely on moral subjects. My subject is—

MORAL INSANITY.

My purpose is to point out some of the symptoms of this insanity. They may be seen in such things as the following:

I. *To live in opposition to the dictates of judgment and conscience.* Man possesses these faculties, and he has also feelings and passions. These often come into conflict with judgment and conscience. Now, it is the part of a rational being to pursue the course which judgment decides is right, and which conscience approves, even if feeling and passion protest ever so strongly against it. This none will deny. But how many blindly follow feeling and passion! This is true of the drunkard, the thief, the covetous, the licentious, and others. Judgment and conscience utter their voice, but feeling and passion prevail. This is a plain symptom of moral insanity.

II. *To be engrossed with the concerns of time, and neglect those of eternity.* What is time? It is that part of duration intervening between the creation of the world and the consummation of all things. This is time in its largest sense. How contracted is that portion of it in which we are concerned! How short the stay of mortals on earth! Many a cradle rocks on the borders of the grave. The young die, the middle-aged, and the old. How short is time! What is eternity? Our feeble powers are unable to grasp the idea. Eternity awaits every child of Adam. Think of countless, measureless ages. Eternity invests all the interests connected with it with tremendous importance. But how many care only for the fleeting interests of time! They pay no attention to the concerns of eternity. This is an undeniable symptom of moral insanity.

III. *To act as if the body was more valuable than the soul.* "What shall we eat? or what shall we drink? or wherewithal shall we be clothed?" are the stereotyped questions transmitted from father to son, and from mother to daughter. They refer to the body. What is the body? A frail mortal thing, to which worms have an inalienable claim, which death will soon enforce. But who can tell the worth of the soul? You may try, and in trying bankrupt the science of numbers, but the value of the soul is incalculable.

> The sun is but a spark of fire,
> A transient meteor in the sky;
> The soul, immortal as its Sire,
> Will never die.

What did Jesus say in Matt. xvi. 26? If the soul is worth more than the whole world, is it not a deplorable symptom of moral insanity to act as if the body was more valuable than the soul?

IV. *To be guilty of practical atheism.* Some deny the existence of God. They are atheists in theory. Many believe in a God, but act as if there was none. They are practical atheists. They commit sins in some places which they would not commit in other places; as if God was not in every place. They do that in secret which they would not do openly. They care not for God. Should they become atheists in theory, they would not live differently. Surely practical atheism indicates moral insanity!

V. *To reject Christ and his salvation.* Jesus Christ came into the world to save sinners. 1 Tim. i. 15. He has procured salvation by his obedience and blood, and this salvation is offered to men without money and without price. Christ is the only Saviour, and his salvation is the only salvation. If he is rejected and his salvation set at naught, there is no hope for guilty men. All rational prospect of eternal life is surrendered. What, then, but the most frightful moral insanity can induce a rejection of Christ and his salvation?

VI. *To intend to be religious at some future time.* If religion deserves attention at all, it deserves attention now. Those who intend to be religious intend to repent—to be sorry for what they are now doing. They purpose to live in sin at present, and to regret in future that they have done so. They are now building up what they intend to pull down. There is nothing but the most alarming insanity that prompts a man to do that *now* of which he intends to repent *in future.*

REMARKS.

I. How prevalent is moral insanity among the rich, the poor, the wise, the ignorant, the old, the young!

II. Let Christians weep over and pray for the morally insane. Their kindred, it may be, are among them.

III. If sinners continue the subjects of this insanity, they will be lost forever. Madness will not only be in their hearts while they live, but after they die, even to all eternity.

SELLING ONE'S SELF INTO SLAVERY.

Thou hast sold thyself to work evil in the sight of the Lord.—1 Kings xxi. 20.

When slavery existed in some of the States of this Union, there were many bad things in the system, but nothing so bad as the power of one man to sell another, to sell mothers and children, thus perpetuating bondage. Happily there is now in this broad land no such slavery. Free men tread the soil everywhere, and the flag of the nation is the symbol of universal liberty. God deserves the praise. But while there is no literal slavery among us, there is something far worse—moral slavery, the slavery of sin. Though men are not selling one another, they are selling themselves. What does the text say? "Thou hast sold thyself." The topic of discussion is—

SELLING ONE'S SELF INTO SLAVERY.

It is well to call attention to—

I. *The nature of this sale.* Several things may be said in illustration of this point.

1. *The person sells himself.* "Thou hast sold thyself." He who sells, is he who is sold. The word "thyself" is full of meaning. It expresses the entire personality—the body and the soul. Thus Ahab sold himself. He sold his body in yielding to his appetites and passions. Many persons now do this. They live to eat and drink. They fall into habits of dissipation. You may see from their appearance that they have sold their bodies. Ahab sold his soul to the slavery of sin. What multitudes copy his example! Indeed, it is the soul that acts through the body, and is committed to the service of sin. It is so sold that all its powers are affected by the sale. The understanding, the judgment, the conscience, the affections, the will, and the imagination, are not what they would have been, had the sale not taken place. To every sinner it may be said, "Thou hast sold thyself."

2. *The sale is voluntary.* There is no compulsion. No man can, as in literal slavery, sell another. Satan can sell no one. He tempts to the making of the sale, but it is with the tempted one to yield. Temptation on the part of Satan shows that he has no coercive power. God himself—I say it with reverence—cannot sell a man into the slavery of sin; in proof of which, I refer to James i. 13. No; man makes the sale, and is voluntary in it. He chooses to make it, thereby desecrating his rational nature, and perverting his moral nature. The literal slave becomes such against his will, the moral slave never. He is not only willing to be sold, but willing to sell himself.

3. *The sale is for purposes of evil.* "Thou hast sold thyself," says the text, "to work evil." This is the design of the sale. "To work evil"—this is a general phrase, including all the forms of evil. These forms are many and diverse, but the evil is expansible into all of them. To work evil, is to act in conflict with the will of God. He who thus works, dishonors God, does harm to himself, and injury to his fellow men. To sell one's self to work evil, is discreditable to hu manity, for it is at war with the best interests of the world.

4. *This work of evil is in the sight of the Lord.* This greatly enhances evil, that it is done in the sight of the Lord. We cannot imagine evil done where the Lord does not see it; but if we could, we would think it less offensive and provoking, than if done before his eyes. All evil, however, is done in the sight of the Lord. Nothing escapes his omniscient glance. You sometimes say to a disobedient child or servant, "Do you dare to disobey me before my face?" Sinners disobey God before his face. They work evil in his sight.

II. *The disgrace of this slavery.* Literal slavery is thought disgraceful, though it is not necessarily so to the slave. If he is forced to be a slave, the dishonor is not on him. The compulsion precludes dishonor. But in the slavery of sin the voluntariness of the bondage makes it disgraceful. It is self-procured slavery. It could have no existence without a rupture of the creature's proper relations to the Creator. Such a rupture clothes him who makes it with disgrace. This slavery is specially disgraceful in view of the love of God manifested in Christ.

III. *The danger of this slavery.* Alas, there is great danger connected with the slavery of sin. This danger may be regarded in two aspects:

1. *The chains of slavery become stronger and stronger.* This results from the law of moral habits. Repetition of evil deeds creates evil habits, and their continued repetition

confirms these habits. We all know something of the power of habit. It is referred to in Jer. xiii. 23. It is dangerous for the chains of moral slavery to grow in strength.

2. *There is danger that these chains may not be broken.* Thanks be to God! in many instances they have been broken, and hence some of us stand to-day on the sacred mount of spiritual emancipation. But how many are there whose bondage is becoming more and more hopeless! We are accustomed to say that while there is life there is hope. I do not think this is universally true. The condition of some sinners is, I suppose, as hopeless before as after they die. I may illustrate by reference to a man above the Falls of Niagara. He may be so far above as to be in no special danger, but he may reach a point when his destruction is as sure as after he makes the fatal plunge. I doubt not there are sinners whose perdition is as certain as if they were now in hell. I do not wish to know who they are.

REMARKS.

I. Many of you, I fear, have sold yourselves.

II. Cry to the Spiritual Emancipator for deliverance from your bondage.

III. There is no hope for you unless you do.

JESUS OFFERED FOR SALE.

What will ye give me, and I will deliver him unto *you?*—Matt. xxvi. 15.

From the infancy of the world selling and buying have been going on. These things are among the operations of commerce—they are commerce. It is human nature to wish to sell at the highest price, and buy at the lowest. Active commerce is the life of the business world. Without it there is stagnation. Many objects are offered for sale, and there are many buyers. Selling and buying are not confined to literal transactions. Judas made a literal sale of Jesus. "What will ye give me?" he covetously asked. Poor man! The sale he made clothed his name with infamy, and no lapse of centuries will take away the stigma. Jesus cannot now be sold in a literal sense, but he is sold in a moral sense—sold virtually every day. This is what we are now to consider.

JESUS OFFERED FOR SALE.

I solicit your attention to the following points:

I. *Many persons sell Jesus.* The economy of the gospel places him in their hands, and they must do something with him. To sell an object is to part with it. This is done by many, so far as Jesus is concerned. They part with him. Look among the rich, and you will see that, with few exceptions, they sell Jesus. They part with him; for they do not want him. There was "no room for him in the inn" when he was born. Alas, these words, "no room" have come down through the centuries and we to-day hear their sad echo.

The poor, too, sell Jesus in the sense of parting with him. In many of the cottages of poverty there is no room for him. The poor are wicked as well as the rich, and they are more numerous. How badly the most of them treat Jesus! Those who are midway between the rich and the poor, that is, those who have a competency, sell Jesus. They part with him. The most of them wish to get clear of him and not to be troubled with him. Thus we see that the circumstances of persons do not prevent their selling Jesus. Nor do their ages. The young, the middle-aged, and the old sell him.

II. *What they take for him.* Poor Judas took thirty pieces of silver. What a bargain! In selling Jesus, men fix on different prices. I name a few of these prices:

1. *A life of ease.* To treat Jesus rightly is to be a Christian,

and to be a Christian is to deny self. This requires earnest, strenuous effort. This we are taught in Matt. vii. 13, 14, and Luke xiii. 24. He who serves Jesus in this world must live a life of unwearied activity. There is no time for ease and sloth. Many persons, however, so love their ease that they neglect salvation. They give themselves no concern about it. They part with Jesus, they sell him, and the price they take is a life of ease. Wretched bargain!

2. *A love of sinful pleasures.* There is no objection to pleasure in itself. The ways of wisdom are ways of pleasantness. But there are what the Bible calls "the pleasures of sin"—that is, such pleasures as cannot be indulged without sinning against God. There are many such pleasures, and their votaries are strangely fascinated. They are so devoted to these pleasures, that they rather part with Jesus than give them up. They sell him; and the enjoyment of "the pleasures of sin for a season" is the price they take. Foolish bargain!

3. *The hope of self-salvation.* There are many persons who admit the importance of salvation, and wish to be saved, but hope to save themselves. They believe, of course, that they are sinners, for this fact makes salvation necessary. They cling, however, to the idea of their own merit. Like the Jews, they try to establish their own righteousness. The moralist relying on his morality, sells Jesus, parts with him, as having no use for him. The more fully the spirit of self-righteousness takes possession of a man, the more promptly does he sell Jesus. He thinks he can do without him, has no use for him. We sell what we think we have no use for. Jesus is sold by all who are deluded with the hope of self-salvation. This is a ruinous bargain.

III. *The wickedness of this sale.* It is great wickedness. This appears in view of such considerations as these:

1. *Who is sold.* It is Jesus, the Son of man, but also the

Son of God. His person is unique. He is the Christ, the God-man, and therefore—

All human beauties, all divine,
In our Beloved meet and shine.

His character is perfect; for in it we see the presence of all excellence, and the absence of all imperfection. This is he who is sold. What wickedness instigates this sale, the sale of the God-man!

2. *The sale involves the basest ingratitude.* Jesus is emphatically the Friend of sinners. The supreme proof of his friendship is found in his incarnation and death. He died for sinners; died for those that sell him. What base ingratitude prompts this sale!

3. *The sale is an insulting depreciation of Jesus in his work of mediation.* How criminal the underestimate placed on him as Mediator, by those who sell him at any price! The wickedness of the sale is inexpressible.

4. *The sale, for whatever price, is moral suicide.* This suicide of the soul is an atrocious sin. The man who sells Jesus brings eternal ruin on himself.

REMARKS.

I. Who of you are selling Jesus?

II. What is the price you are taking for him?

III. I demand justice for him, and call on you to stop the sale, and stop it now.

CHRIST DESPISED AND REJECTED.

He is despised and rejected of men.—Isa. liii. 3.

We are at no loss to know who is referred to in these words. In different parts of the New Testament this connection of Scripture is said to have received its fulfillment in Christ. Things are said in this chapter which are true of

Christ alone. They cannot refer to any other being in the universe. When he appeared on earth in the flesh, men saw "no beauty in him." Instead of being attracted to him they were repelled from him. Since his death and ascension to glory also there are multitudes who hate and reject him. It is therefore appropriate to dwell on the topic that I now present—

CHRIST DESPISED AND REJECTED.

Let us notice—

I. *Who is despised and rejected?* I may say, in answer to this question—

1. *The Son of God.* This phrase is of frequent occurrence in the Scriptures, and it plainly denotes a special relation to God. Indeed, Christ is termed the only-begotten Son, which shows that the relation is unique, exemplified in Christ alone. It is in a far inferior sense that Christians are made sons of God, and they are so made through the mediation of Christ. He, however, is the Son of God in the exalted sense which implies that all divine perfections are his. The Jews understood him, in declaring himself the Son of God, to make himself equal with God, and he tacitly admitted it. He is the Son of God, truly divine. See Col. ii. 9.

2. *The Son of man.* This phrase denotes a human relation as certainly as the phrase, Son of God, expresses a divine relation. Christ is the Son of Mary, " born of a woman," the woman belonging to the human race. He is therefore related to universal humanity. His assumption of our nature makes him the brother of our race, places him on an equality with every other man, in the possession of a common nature. Here the equality stops; for, as to character, he is "separate from sinners." The union of the two natures in his person constitutes him the Christ.

3. *The Saviour of sinners.* The Son of God becoming the

Son of man of necessity became the God-man. As the God man he is the Saviour. An atoning death, and therefore a death by substitution, was indispensable to his becoming a Saviour. He must be man to make it possible for him to die, and he must be God to make it possible for him to die as a substitute. Because he thus died he is *a* Saviour, *the* Saviour, the *only* Saviour of sinners. This is the Being who is despised and rejected—*the Son of God, the Son of man, the Saviour of sinners.* Oh, think of it, and let us see—

II. *By whom he is despised and rejected.* The text says "of men," that is, by men. This great sin, specially the sin of rejection, can be committed by human beings only. The Devil and demons hate Christ, but they do not reject him. To reject implies an offer which is refused. Christ is not offered as a Saviour to Satan and his angels. No, the offer is made to men, and human beings alone are capable of the awful distinction which a rejection of Christ gives. This highest conspicuity in guilt is theirs exclusively. For Christ to be despised and rejected by men is most unreasonable and wicked. This is seen in view of—

1. *The loveliness of his character.* There is in this character a most attractive combination of divine and human excellences. It is altogether lovely. To despise such a character and reject such a Being, is most unreasonable and wicked. It is to despise infinite loveliness and to reject him in whom that loveliness is exemplified.

2. *What Christ has done for men.* What has he done? To form the best idea that we can of it, we must consider the height of his glory and the depth of his humiliation, looking at all he did in leaving that height and descending to that depth. We begin with his incarnation; then we come to his life of sorrow, his agony in the garden, his death on the cross, and his burial in Joseph's tomb. From the tomb he rose and ascended to heaven, to preside over the accomplishment of the

objects he had in view when he died. All this was for **men**; and they reject him!

3. *What Christ has said to men.* Referring to himself as the source whence flow the waters of salvation, he has said, in the audience of the world, "If any man thirst, let him come to me and drink." He has commanded the gospel to be preached in all the world, to every creature. He has promised salvation to all who are willing to be saved by him. All this is said to men. There is no offer of salvation to fallen angels, but to fallen men. How unreasonable and wicked for men to despise and reject Christ!

III. *The consequences resulting.* If the despising and the rejection are persisted in, what follows?

1. *Men remain unsaved.* They are condemned already. There is no way of deliverance but through Christ. If therefore he is rejected, there is no deliverance. The despisers and rejecters of Christ remain unsaved. What a wretched state is this!

2. *Aggravated guilt is incurred.* "Unto whomsoever much is given, of him shall be much required." Much is given when Christ is given to the world as the Saviour. He is God's great gift to men. To reject him is the great sin, the guilt of which it will require eternity to comprehend.

3. *Utter ruin follows.* It follows the guilt with inevitable certainty. What say the Scriptures? Luke xiii. 3; John viii. 24; 2 Thess. i. 7-9; Heb. x. 29. Divine wrath, in its severest manifestations, awaits the despisers and rejecters of Christ. What will poor sinners do when God calls them to account for rejecting his Son?

REMARKS.

I. Are you guilty of this great sin?

II. If so, repent of it and cry to God for mercy.

III. There is no hope for you unless you do.

PROCRASTINATION.

Go thy way for this time ; when I have a convenient season I will call for thee.—Acts xxiv. 25.

Paul stood before Felix and "reasoned of righteousness, temperance, and judgment to come." He made a wise selection of topics. He discoursed on righteousness, in the presence of an unrighteous man; on temperance, in the presence of a man who practiced very little self-restraint; and at a judgment seat where justice had very often been disregarded, he spoke of a judgment to come, in which there will be the strictest adherence to equity. A strange scene was presented. The governor-judge trembled, the prisoner was calm. Felix trembled and said: "Go thy way for this time." My topic is—

PROCRASTINATION.

I present the following points:

I. *The folly of procrastination.* Folly is the opposite of wisdom, and appears manifest in contrast with it. It is the part of wisdom to bestow on every subject attention proportionate to its importance. What subject is so important as salvation? But the language of procrastination is, that salvation, though important, is not important *now;* that preparation for eternity need not be made *at present;* and that it will do to care for the soul at some future time. Does not this indicate folly? Men do not act in this way in worldly matters. When they buy farms, they do not say: "Those of whom we have bought have many years to live, and there is time enough to secure deeds and titles." They are not willing to risk even a little property on the continuance of their neighbors' lives, but they will risk their eternal interests on the continuance of their own lives. Is not this folly? The swine that trample pearls under their feet do not act so foolishly.

Again, those who intend at some future time to become Christians intend to repent; for they know that repentance is indispensable. They therefore virtually say, "We will sin now, but will be sorry for it in time to come." That is, they are now building up what they fully intend to pull down by-and-by. They are walking in the ways of sin, but it is their purpose, after a while, to retrace their steps with grief and tears. If this is not folly, we may as well expunge the term from our language. It will never be more applicable to any subject.

II. *The delusiveness of procrastination.* Sinners deceive themselves in supposing that they will become Christians at some future time. Satan himself does not object to this view, for he uses it as an opiate for the conscience. How do they know that they will become Christians at some future day? They imagine that there are difficulties in the way now that will be obviated in time to come. How do they know? Can they pry into futurity and tell what is to be and not to be? Are they not deluded? As to difficulties, they will be as great in all time to come as they are now. A heathen poet refers to a rustic who on the river bank "expectant stands until the stream rolls by." Under as great delusion labors the man who, on account of present difficulties, is deterred from seeking the salvation of his soul. Is not the spirit of procrastination a delusive spirit?

III. *The guilt of procrastination.* It is sinful to delay repentance. Two facts will make this evident:

1. *Those who procrastinate promise to give to God what does not belong to them.* I mean future time. Time is so valuable that God gives it to us by moments. You cannot say that any moment except the present is yours. You are dishonest in promising to give to God what does not belong to you. Suppose I should promise to give away your property: you would say I had no right to do so, the property not being

mine. But I would have the same right that you have to give future time to God—that is, none at all. When you make such a promise you both presume on the future, and sin against God by agreeing to give to him what is not your own.

2. *God forbids procrastination.* He does this in commanding sinners to repent. I assume it as a fact that you are under obligation to God. You admit this by intending to repent. If then you are under obligation to obey God, you are guilty when you disobey him. What does he say to you? See Isa. lv. 6, 7; Matt. vii. 13; Luke xiv. 17; Heb. iii. 7; Rev. xxii. 17. Every moment you put off your return to God you sin against him. The delay is sinful. Is there not guilt in procrastination?

IV. *The danger of procrastination.* There is danger—

1. *Because of the power of sinful habits.* Every one knows that habits, good or bad, can be confirmed. The more a man sins against God, the more the habit of sinning is confirmed. Jer. xiii. 23. The more one sins, the more is he inclined to sin. The power of sinful habits creates great danger.

2. *Because God may give up sinners to work out their destruction.* When God says to a man, as he did to Ephraim, "Let him alone," what hope is there? The time of the Jews' visitation passed away unimproved, and their house was left desolate. The means of grace are a curse when God withholds his blessing.

3. *Because death is at hand.* Death ends the day of mercy. There is no salvation offered to the dead. When death comes, the sinner's character becomes hopelessly unchangeable.

REMARKS.

I. Do not copy the example of Felix.

II. It will require eternity to comprehend the folly, the delusiveness, the guilt, and the danger of procrastination.

THE SIN OF INGRATITUDE.

But Hezekiah rendered not again according to the benefit done unto him.—2 Chron. xxxii. 25.

Hezekiah was reckoned among the good kings of Judah. This is remarkable, as his father Ahaz, and his son Manasseh, were very wicked. History often teaches us that piety has no necessary connection with lineal descent. We are reminded that the Lord's servants are "born, not of blood . . . . but of God." John i. 13. The two most conspicuous facts in the life of Hezekiah were his miraculous rescue from the ruin threatened to his kingdom by Sennacherib, King of Assyria, and his wonderful recovery from sickness, with fifteen years added to his life. He no doubt felt at the time profoundly grateful for these deliverances; but he soon forgot them. He was like the children of Israel after they crossed the Red Sea. Psalm cvi. 13. The theme suggested by the words of the text is—

THE SIN OF INGRATITUDE.

Let us inquire into—

I. *The nature of ingratitude.* What is it? It is a failure to appreciate kindness. It is not to feel obligations created by favors received. It is to be unthankful for benefits conferred. It is, of course, the opposite of gratitude. The obligations of gratitude are regulated by the relations of parties to one another. These obligations exist where parties are equal. They are stronger when the party conferring the favor is superior in position, in character, and in reputation, and where the party receiving is very unworthy. Apply this principle to the relation between God and man. He is highly exalted above all his creatures. When he bestows blessings on them, there should be devout appreciation. This is true of all rational creatures; but men are sinful creatures, and their unworthiness results from this fact. Their obligations to be grateful are stronger because of their unworthiness. Ingratitude does not recognize these obligations at all. The ungrateful heart is an insensible heart, a callous heart, a heart without feeling.

II. *The sin of ingratitude.* "Hezekiah rendered not again acording to the benefit done unto him." He had received signal blessings. His ingratitude was sinful, and strikingly unreasonable in view of what God had done for him. That we may be impressed with the sin of our ingratitude, let us consider what benefits we have received from God.

1. *Our providential mercies.* These are many, and they all come from God. He has brought us into the world at the most favored period of the world's history. What past century was so full of interest as the present? God has placed us on the theatre of life at this time. He has given us our abode in the most desirable part of the world. He has given us food and clothing. Speaking in general terms, we can say, that we have lacked nothing. We have many physical comforts, many intellectual pleasures, and many moral advantages; but how ungrateful we are as compared with what we should be! Some of you, perhaps, never have a feeling of gratitude to God. You lie down at night with no gratitude for the blessings of the day, and rise up in the morning with no praises on your lips. You forget God. He has infinite claims on your remembrance. His favors should be thankfully received; but you are like Hezekiah. Is not ingratitude a sin?

2. *God has given his Son to die for us.* This is the wonder of the universe. Well is it said: "Herein is love, not that we loved God, but that he loved us, and sent his Son to be the propitiation for our sins." 1 John iv. 10. The proof of this love is overwhelming. No angel can conceive how stronger proof could be given. God, in giving his Son

to die, had in view the salvation of men. He designed to link their salvation inseparably with his glory. In order to this, Jesus must die an atoning death. His blood must be sacrificially poured forth. The cross presents the only hope for lost sinners; but how many reject Christ! What ingratitude! How base! How atrocious! Those who do not gladly accept God's offer of Christ as a Saviour, are monsters in human form. Satan may tempt them to commit this great sin, but he does not commit it. The ingratitude is worse than Satanic.

3. *God has made many of us his children.* He has called us by his grace out of darkness into light. He has subdued our enmity, and made us his friends. He has delivered us from spiritual death, and made us subjects of spiritual life. By regeneration he has given us the nature of children, and by adoption the name of "sons and daughters," so that we cry "Abba, Father." He has forgiven all our sins. How much he has done for us! What have we rendered to him? Are we free from the sin of ingratitude? Ah no; we have not rendered according to the benefit done to us.

4. *God has given us the hope of heaven.* It would be a great thing if he should let us live on earth always, as his children, with trials and afflictions as now; but he is going to do for us far better than this. The hope of glory he has given us is to be realized. Immortal blessedness is promised us, and the promise is sure. What are we rendering to God for the hope he has given us? Does not the charge of in gratitude lie against us?

REMARKS.

I. There is no baser sin than ingratitude.

II. Let sinners and saints repent of it.

III. Render to God from this hour according to his benefits.

NO EXCUSE FOR SIN.

If I had not come and spoken unto them, they had not had sin: but now they have no cloak for their *sin*.—John xv. 22.

Where little is given little is required, and where much is given much is required. These principles, so manifestly just, were announced by Christ, and are everywhere recognized in the gospel. They will be recognized in the judgment of the last day. The difference between little and much is so great that those receiving little are comparatively without responsibility and without guilt. It is only comparatively, not really. This is the meaning of the text—that in a comparative sense, men would not have sinned if Christ had not come; that is, they would not have had it in their power to sin in circumstances so aggravated. The topic now to be considered is this:

NO EXCUSE FOR SIN.

To illustrate this topic, I present the following points:

I. *Christ has come and spoken to men.* "If I had not come and spoken unto them." The advent of Christ in the flesh introduced a new era. We say the Christian era, dating it from the birth of Christ. "In the year of our Lord," is a common form of expression. Christ came in fulfillment of prophecy. His coming was looked for during a period of four thousand years. Every sacrifice anticipated it; the blood of every altar ran in the direction of Calvary. The coming of Christ is the most important of all events. How benevolent the object for which he came! John x. 10; 1 Tim. i. 15. Christ has spoken to men. On what subject? Not about the trifles of this world. He has not told us how to get wealth, or honor, or any worldly thing. He has told us about God, revealing the divine character. He has told us of our sin and condemnation, our helpless guilt and guilty helplessness. He has told us the way of salvation. He has told us of a glorious heaven, and how to obtain it. He has told us of a fearful hell, and how to avoid it. How thankful ought men to be that Jesus has come and spoken to them!

II. *If Jesus had not come and spoken to men, they would not have had sin, comparatively.* How much less would they have known of God and salvation! Christ came as the Light of the world. If he had not come, the world would have remained in darkness. He came as the Life of the world. Had he not come, the world would have continued in death. He came as the Saviour of the world. If he had not come, there would have been no salvation. By his coming he abolished death, and brought immortal life to light through the gospel. How different the condition of those living before, and those living after, the coming of Christ! How little light was enjoyed in patriarchal times, and under the Mosaic Economy! Sin committed then was not sin, as compared with sin committed now. The light then was darkness, as compared with the light now. It is a startling thought, that while the coming of Christ secures the salvation of countless millions, it makes it possible for men to sin far more inexcusably than if he had not come. To perish through a refusal to use a remedy is far worse than to perish because there is no remedy. You now have some faint idea of what Jesus meant by saying that men would have had no sin if he had not come and spoken to them. That is, they would have had no sin comparatively.

III. *Now men have no excuse for sin.* The text says, "no cloak." A cloak is a covering, something used to cover. Figuratively, it is a pretext, an excuse. To have no cloak for sin is to have no excuse for it. Those who reject Christ are in this condition. What excuse can they make for their sin? None that will possess a single element of validity at the judgment. They sin against light; for "to them who sit in darkness has light sprung up." Matt. iv. 16. It is light from heaven, lighting every man that comes into the world. Men sin against this light. Is there any excuse for it? They sin against knowledge. They *know* far more and far better than they *do*. They do not sin ignorantly, but knowingly. What excuse have they? They sin against love. There was an incarnation of love when Jesus became incarnate. It was love that brought him down from heaven. It was love that made him the Man of sorrows. It was love that sought vocal expression when he said, "My soul is exceeding sorrowful, even unto death." It was love that presided over the scene of crucifixion and gladly exclaimed, "It is finished." There is no love like this. But men sin against it. What excuse have they? Is there the shadow of justification? They sin against atoning blood. Without this blood there is no remission of sins; and, therefore, to sin against it is a suicidal thing. It ruins the soul. It makes the sinner the author of his miserable destiny. Think of the value of the blood sinned against—the blood of Christ. They sin against mediatorial authority. Jesus as Mediator has all power, and a name above every name. Phil. ii. 8–11. Rejection of Christ is the climax of sin, for which there is no excuse.

REMARKS.

I. Your attempts to make excuse for your sin are vain.

II. You will make no excuse at the judgment seat.

III. Let not the coming of Christ be the means of aggravating your perdition.

THE OFFICE OF THE LAW.

Wherefore the law was our school-master to bring us unto Christ, that we might be justified by faith.—Gal. iii. 24.

Paul, in his Epistles to the Romans and Galatians, uses the term law to denote the ceremonial law of the Jews, and also the moral law, peculiar to neither Jews nor Gentiles, but common to both. In Romans iii. 21, he refers to the former, and in verse 19, to the latter. In the second verse of the chapter from which the text is taken, the ceremonial law is no doubt meant, while in verse 13, the moral law is referred to. In Romans x. 4, I rather think the term law is employed in its twofold sense; and this I take to be its import in the text. Probably the meaning is, the system of law, including the law ceremonial and the law moral, was our school-master. The subject to consider is—

THE OFFICE OF THE LAW.

What is it? The text tells us—

I. *To lead to Christ.*

1. *This was true of the ceremonial law.* One of the most prominent features of this law was the offering of sacrifices. In these sacrifices there was a symbolic transfer of sin from the offerer to the victim. The guilty man placed his hand on the head of the victim. This was an individual sacrifice. In general sacrifices the high priest acted for the congregation of Israel. Now the symbolic transfer of guilt was of course not a real transfer, but it was typical of a real transfer to be made when the Lamb of God should present himself at the altar of sacrifice on Calvary. In this sense the ceremonial law was a school-master to lead to Christ. This was its office, and its types and shadows were fulfilled in him.

2. *Supremely true of the moral law.* This law lays its claims imperatively on all rational creatures. The ceremonial law of the Jews is done away; but the moral law, existing before the ceremonial, still exists, and will exist forever. The whole of this law is virtually compressed by Christ into the two requirements of love to God and love to men, and these are vitally incorporated into the gospel. It is the office of the moral law to lead to Christ. It does this—

a By showing what sin is. "Where no law is there is no transgression." "For sin is the transgression of the law." It is also said: "By the law is the knowledge of sin." This is because the law is the standard of right. It is spiritual, reaching the heart as well as the life. The law makes every man know that he is a sinner, because it shows what sin is, and he sees that he has committed it in violating his obligations to God. This knowledge of sin is the first step taken in the way that leads to Christ. If this step is not taken, no other will be taken.

b. By revealing the danger to which sin exposes. The danger is seen in the penalty of the law. As sin is no trifle, but a terrible evil, the peril to which the sinner is liable is fearful. This peril includes all that is meant by the wrath of God. This wrath is revealed (Rom. i. 18; Eph. v. 6), and it abides even now on the unbeliever (John iii. 36), but it is in a special sense the wrath to come. Are not transgressors of the law exposed to terrific danger? Unquestionably. A knowledge of this danger is a second step in the way that leads to Christ. A sense of the need of Christ as a Saviour is connected with a knowledge of the danger to which sin, as the transgression of the law, exposes.

c. By destroying all hope of legal justification. This hope is entertained by all who do not know what sin is, and the danger to which it exposes. There is in man an innate partiality for the doctrine of justification by works. All are Pharisees by nature. Those who become Christians die to the law. They die to all hope of justification by works of law. This is true of any kind of law and any kind of works. This species of death is indispensable to discipleship to Christ. No one lives to God who does not first die to the law. What said Paul of himself? "I through the law died to the law, that I might live unto God." Gal. ii. 19, Revised Version. The law makes no compromises, but requires perfect and perpetual obedience. Legal justification is impossible unless man can do more than the law requires, so that present and future obedience may make up for past failures. But this can never be, for the good reason that man cannot at any time do more than his duty. The law, with its holiness, its spirituality, and its penalty, properly understood, crucifies all hope of salvation by works. In destroying this hope, the law does not leave the sinner hopeless, but leads him to Christ for salvation. It leads him away from the deeds of the law to the grace of the gospel. In short, it drives him from Sinai and leads him to Calvary.

II. *What occurs when the law performs its office.* This the text leaves in no doubt; for it says, "that we might be justified by faith." If we understand the system of faith which the gospel reveals to be referred to, this is the only way of justification. We are justified by grace through the redemption that is in Christ Jesus. If we understand faith as that act of the soul that receives Christ and relies on him for salvation, it is in this sense the indispensable means of justification. How suitable this way of justification! No other way would be suitable or possible. "It is of faith, that it might be by grace." In the gospel method of salvation, grace and faith are adjusted to each other.

REMARKS.

I. It is all-important that the law perform its office.

II. The law should be preached in the gospel.

III. Pitiable are those who rely on works of law for salvation.

THE GREATNESS OF THE SIN OF UNBELIEF.

But he that believeth not is condemned already, because he hath not believed in the name of the only-begotten Son of God.—John iii. 18.

There is no chapter in the Bible which contains more important and more precious truth than this. We have here in substance the whole gospel of the grace of God. We are told of the two great things in a sinner's salvation which involve whatever accompanies salvation. These two things are regeneration by the Holy Spirit, and faith in the Son of God. What Jesus said to Nicodemus on these points is, I trust, familiar to most of you. The subject of faith has connection with the gift and the mission of Christ, as we see from verses 14–18. God gave his Son, and faith receives him, while unbelief rejects him. It is implied that some believe and others do not. Not to believe in Christ must be a great sin. Hence the topic for present discussion—

THE GREATNESS OF THE SIN OF UNBELIEF.

That unbelief is a great sin will appear from these two facts—

I. *It entails condemnation.* I use the word entails with a purpose. It means, in law, to settle or fix, but there must first be something to settle or fix. To entail, therefore, is not to originate the thing entailed. So it is with unbelief. It does not originate a sinner's condemnation, but it settles, intensifies, and perpetuates it. To make this matter plain, I need only say, that a transgression of God's law is the original basis on which condemnation rests. Unbelief rejects the gospel. But there would have been no gospel and no need of any, if sinners had not been condemned by the law. The essence of the gospel is that it tells the way of deliverance from the condemnation of the law. Nor is the law-basis of condemnation by any means narrow. It is so wide that the whole world stands on it, condemnation being universal. We are taught (Rom. i. 18–20) that the heathen are without excuse. This shows that they are justly condemned. Moral obligation is recognized in the law of nature, but more fully in the written "law and the prophets." Hence the Jews were more inexcusable than the Gentiles. When Jesus gave the commission (Mark xvi. 15, 16), he meant that all men were lost, condemned, and in need of salvation. While a violation of law is the basis of condemnation, unbelief, in its rejection of the gospel, entails and greatly aggravates it. The text says, "He that believeth not is condemned already"—literally, *has been condemned.* This condemnation remains because of unbelief. How great then must be the sin of unbelief! For we are to remember that the salvation of the gospel, if accepted, brings glory to God, in the highest sense of the term glory, and also secures the best interests of men. When unbelief rejects the salvation, God is dishonored and insulted. What he has done in providing a Saviour is contemptuously treated. Is not this a great sin? Those, too, who continue in unbelief do their souls fatal injury. Prov. viii. 36. No man has the right to do this. It is a great sin; but all that I have said is involved in the sin of unbelief. Hence I argue the greatness of this sin. It is better to use the concrete than the abstract. I say, then, that the sin of the unbeliever is great, or in other words, that the unbeliever is a great sinner.

2. *It rejects the only begotten Son of God.* "Because he hath not believed in the name of the only begotten Son of God." This implies that not to believe in Christ is a sin of no ordinary magnitude. I beg you to notice the phrase "*Son of God.*" It denotes a relation to God which, in some respects, is like that between an earthly son and father; but, in other respects, infinitely unlike. The second person in the Trinity was the Son of God from eternity. You say you cannot comprehend this; nor can I. But God sent his Son, and he must have been his Son before he sent him. Notice the words "*only begotten.*" One Son, unique, infinitely beloved, and, speaking after the manner of men, we may say, more beloved because the only Son. Now God so loved the world as to give this "only begotten Son." In giving him he so

exhausted the treasury of heaven that he has never given anything else except in connection with him and for his sake. This "only begotten Son of God" became the Son of man, the Son of Mary became a Man of sorrows, the object of malicious hate, at whom calumny shot all the arrows in its quiver. He died for sins, because he died for sinners. His death was indispensable to salvation. No ray of light or hope reaches man in his darkness that does not emanate from the cross. Acts iv. 12. Salvation was procured by his obedience and blood. This dearly bought salvation is offered to men "without money and without price." But unbelievers will not accept it. They reject the only Saviour. Here the sinfulness of unbelief is seen. Here we perceive what Jesus means in John xvi. 9. The Holy Spirit, in convincing of sin, directs attention to sin in its most aggravated form, even as it appears in the rejection of the Saviour. Faith in Christ is the appropriation of the only remedy for the removal of the disease of sin. Unbelief will have nothing to do with the remedy. It is, therefore, a most peculiar sin and the greatest of sins, because it infallibly prevents the pardon of all other sins. Consider this: Here are other sins without number, and, according to the gospel, they might all be pardoned in a moment but for unbelief. This great sin hinders the application of the remedy for the removal of sin. It refuses to accept Christ, the only begotten Son of God. The essence of its demerit and turpitude is to be found in its rejection of the only Saviour of sinners.

REMARKS.

I. We see the perilous condition of unbelievers.

II. The only hope for them is in repenting and believing the gospel. The consequences of final unbelief will be dreadful. John viii. 24.

SATAN AN ANGEL OF LIGHT.

For Satan himself is transformed into an angel of light.—2 Cor. xi. 14

Everything good is counterfeited. Pride apes humility; ignorance clothes itself in the garb of wisdom; hypocrisy feigns to be sincere; enmity rankles under the mask of friendship. Strange to say, there were false apostles when Paul wrote this letter to the Corinthians. Men of this class are referred to in Revelation ii. 2. The church at Ephesus tested their claims, and exposed their pretensions. It is difficult now to say what motives prompted those false apostles to transform themselves into the apostles of Christ; but the text gives the reason why the transformation was not to be marveled at. "For Satan himself is transformed into an angel of light." My subject will be—

SATAN AN ANGEL OF LIGHT.

My first inquiry will be—

I. *Who is Satan?* The name is significant, meaning *adversary, enemy.* It is usually applied to the evil being we call the Devil. This fallen spirit is the chief of the fallen angels. Matt. xxv. 41. He has various appellations. John xii. 31; Eph. ii. 2; 2 Cor. iv. 4; 1 Peter v. 8; 1 John v. 18; Rev. xx. 2. The plural, devils, should be *demons.* There are many demons, while there is but one devil. Satan is the adversary of God and of man. He is full of malignity. What he did before his work in Eden, we know not; but he has been busily engaged ever since. The lapse of centuries does not exhaust his malignity. He is a powerful, crafty, and persevering enemy. His enmity to God makes him the enemy of all the creatures of God. He is intent on the destruction of creatures and the defeat of the divine plans. He wields the forces of evil, and they are immense.

II. *How does Satan transform himself into an angel of light?* We learn from the context that the "false apostles" transformed themselves. They pretended to be what they were not. Under the guise of virtue they acted wickedly. Satan transforms himself. An angel of light is a good angel. Satan therefore pretends to be a good angel. He assumes to be the patron of truth and righteousness. Let me illustrate as follows: I refer to—

1. *The temptation in Eden.* This was Satan's first transformation in this world. Gen. iii. 1–5. He pretended to be the special friend of our mother Eve. He insisted that great advantage would result from eating of the fruit of the tree of knowledge. "Ye shall be as gods, knowing good and evil." There was to be a vast enlargement of the realm of knowledge. He did not intimate that any evil consequences would follow.

2. *The temptation of Christ.* We have an account of this in Matthew iv. 1–11, and Luke iv. 1–13. According to Luke, Christ was tempted for forty days. Matthew tells us that at the end of forty days he was hungry, and Satan presented three temptations. There is no contradiction. Jesus was tempted for forty days, and the three temptations recorded were the last of the series. In these three, and doubtless in all, Satan appeared as an angel of light. He seemed anxious for Christ to act in a way worthy of his dignity as the Son of God. How plausible was the implication that it would be best for the interests of his kingdom if Christ, in the beginning of his ministry, would give open proof of his Divine Sonship! Satan artfully pretended to be the advocate of Christ's claims to the Messiahship, and said nothing as to the design of his temptations.

3. *Advocacy of sound doctrine.* Satan as an angel of light appears to be zealous for the truth. We may well believe that he instigated Arius to assign Christ a place above all creatures, but not to admit his equality with God. Afterward he gave Christ a lower place, and then a still

lower, admitting him at last to be a very good man. In all this, Satan claims to be an angel of light, jealous lest God should be defrauded of his glory. A denial of the doctrine of atonement is based on what Satan suggests are proper views of the character of God. It is asked: "Does God need to be propitiated? Is he not love?" Regeneration by the Holy Spirit is supposed to be a reflection on the integrity of human nature. "Did not God make man?" says Satan. "Did he not do his work well?" If Satan cannot induce the belief that regeneration is needless, then he insinuates that baptism regenerates, that "sacraments" have efficacy, that we must come to Christ through the church, and through priests. Satan, under pretence of zeal for the maintenance of truth, favors union of Church and State.

4. *He makes what is wrong appear right, and what is bad appear good.*

a. He makes pride seem to be dignity He gets the advantange of many Christians in this way. They do foolish things, supposing that they are maintaining dignity of character. They are prompted by pride in what they do.

b. He makes resentment and a refusal to forgive injuries appear to be self-respect. It is well to have proper self-respect, but it is not be confounded with resentment and revenge. What some professors of religion call *self-respect* is a great hindrance to the spirituality of many churches. It prevents the adjustment of differences among brethren, and, in many ways, does immense harm.

c. He makes covetousness seem a wise provision for the future. Parents say, that they must lay up something for their children. This is right, but it is not to be so done as to rob the cause of God. There are few sins more deeply rooted than the sin of covetousness; but when Satan as an angel of light defines it he makes it appear commendable.

d. He makes worldly conformity seem the best means of ex-

erting a religious influence over worldly persons. This is a great mistake, but Satan conceals it.

e. He makes it appear best for the young to wait till their minds become mature before they become religious, and for those in active life to retire from business before they concern themselves about salvation.

f. He makes despair of mercy appear to be humility. If he cannot prevent a sinner from seeking salvation, then he will say "there is no hope, and true humility is despair." Thus effort is paralyzed, and there is no striving "to enter in at the strait gate."

REMARKS.

I. Satan as an enemy is most dangerous as an angel of light.

II. Christians, your safety is in watching and prayer.

III. O sinners, let not Satan retain you as his captives.

IV. Satanic power yields to divine omnipotence.

THE DISEASE AND THE PHYSICIAN.

Is there no balm in Gilead? Is there no physician there? Why then is not the health of the daughter of my people recovered?—Jer. viii. 22.

In this text the Jewish nation is represented as afflicted with a dire disease. Pursuing the figure, the prophet inquires, "Is there no balm in Gilead?" Balm was in those days largely used in the healing art, and Gilead furnished an abundant supply. The prophet virtually says, "My people are diseased. Is there no remedy? If there is a remedy, is there no physician to apply it?" Isaiah refers to the same disease in the words, "The whole head is sick." Isa. i. 5, 6. Christ employs the same metaphor. Matt. ix. 12. I am justified therefore in discoursing on—

THE DISEASE AND THE PHYSICIAN.

I may surely say that—

I. *Man is the subject of moral disease.* The common name for this disease is sin, and the metaphor has its basis in the fact that sin affects the moral constitution, even as literal disease affects the physical frame. The malignity of this moral disease may be referred to in connection with—

1. *Its antiquity.* It is an old disease. Its ravages began with the birth of sin. As soon as man ate the forbidden fruit this disease assailed his moral constitution, and all its organs at once ceased to perform their appropriate functions.

2. *Its universality.* It has been as wide-spread as the human race. It has prevailed in every land, on every sea, under every form of government, and in every generation.

3. *Its incurableness by human means.* Philosophers have made their experiments. They have been to some extent acquainted with the disease, but have never discovered a remedy. It has been supposed by some that the culture of the intellect would remove the disease; but the disease is of the heart, and intellectual culture has never made the heart what it should be.

II. *The competency of the Physician.* Christ is the Physician of souls. He is altogether competent, because—

1. *He is omniscient.* He is therefore acquainted with the pathology of the case, and knows what remedy is needed and how to apply it.

2. *He has provided a remedy.* It may be called a twofold remedy, made up of atoning blood and regenerating grace.

3. *He is skillful in the application of the remedy.* He has had adequate experience. Proofs of his skill are to be found in all the centuries.

4. *He is sympathizing and faithful.* He pities his diseased patients and does not let them suffer for lack of his attention.

5. *He is unconfined to localities.* The physician of the body may lose a patient because he is in some other place, and can be in but one place at a time. Christ, the Physician of souls, is in all places. No diseased sinner is where Christ is not; for he is everywhere.

III. *The importance of an immediate application to the Physician.*

Three things make this evident—

1. *The disease is progressive in its tendency.* It is constantly becoming worse, and more deeply seated. The sooner the Physician is called to apply the remedy the better.

2. *The Physician says, "Now is the accepted time."* He knows when the remedy can be best applied.

3. *Delay has ruined millions.* The only safe thing for the diseased sinner to do is to apply to the Physician at once.

REMARKS.

I. Those saved from this disease are under infinite obligations to the Great Physician.

II. They should feel deep concern for their diseased fellow-creatures.

III. They should most earnestly recommend the Physician by saying, "He has healed us, and he can heal others."

IV. If the disease results in eternal death, the blame will rest on the diseased. There is a remedy, and a Physician to apply it. Relief is gratuitously afforded.

SIN WRONGS THE SOUL

But he that sinneth against me wrongeth his own soul.—Prov. viii. 36.

Men often wrong one another. This is true of individuals and of nations. For what are courts of justice established? Is it not that wrongs inflicted on persons and on communities may be remedied? In war, nations wrong one another on a large scale. All history shows this. But do men ever wrong themselves? Nothing is more common. They wrong themselves more frequently than they do their fellow-men. Every wrong done to others is a wrong to themselves, and some of their sins are an injury to themselves alone.

I shall attempt, on this occasion, to establish this proposition—

SIN WRONGS THE SOUL.

You will observe that I speak not of the injury sin does to the body, but to the soul. We have many proofs that sin wrongs the body; but the most appalling injury it inflicts is on the soul. How does it wrong the soul?

I. *The effect it produces on the soul's faculties shows its injurious influence.*

Consider in proof of this the following points—

1. *Sin darkens the understanding.* Paul uses these words: "Having the understanding darkened, being alienated from the life of God through the ignorance that is in them, because of the blindness of their heart." Eph. iv. 18. The heart is the seat of depravity and exerts an injurious influence on the intellect. Hence, "the eyes of your understanding" need to be enlightened.

2. *It warps the judgment.* Amid the darkness of the understanding the judgment gives wrong decisions. Men may reach the point at which they will call good evil, and evil good. They may confound the distinction between truth and error.

3. *It stupefies the conscience.* It is the special province of conscience to approve and condemn in accordance with the decisions of the judgment. Hence it indirectly stimulates to the doing of that which it can approve, and deters from the doing of that which it must condemn. But sin sears the con-

science "with a hot iron," that is, benumbs its sensibilities. Stupefaction of conscience is a deplorable calamity.

4. *It perverts the will.* The will of a holy being coincides perfectly with the will of God. Sin causes the will of the creature to come into conflict with the will of the Creator. This conflict has to do with the very essence of sin.

5. *It desecrates the affections.* It withdraws them from God and induces a violation of "the first and great commandment" of the law, "Thou shalt love the Lord thy God with all thy heart." No language can describe the great wrong sin does the soul in the desecration of its affections.

6. *It corrupts the imagination.* This imperial faculty, instead of soaring among the works and wonders of creation, providence, and redemption, grovels amid contaminating worldly influences.

Thus does it appear that sin wrongs the soul by its injurious influence on the soul's faculties.

II. *Sin deprives the soul of happiness.* "There is no peace, saith my God, to the wicked." Happiness is that state of the soul in which all its desires are gratified. But they can never be gratified while the soul is at war with the plans and purposes of God. Man was created that he might "glorify God and enjoy him forever." To enjoy God, to be happy in him, was one of the purposes of man's creation. Nor can happiness be found apart from God. The experiment has been made numberless times, but it has always failed and always will fail. Happiness is possible to the soul of man through fellowship with God, and in no other way. Those who seek it otherwise have forsaken "the fountain of living waters, and hewed them out cisterns, broken cisterns, that can hold no water." Jer. ii. 13. Sin, in prompting the soul's departure from God, deprives it of happiness, and thus does it a wrong of great magnitude.

III. *Sin unfits the soul for heaven.* Heaven is a holy

place, for it is, in a special sense, the dwelling-place of God. The joy of heaven is holy joy, and its society is holy. The pure in heart see God, and without holiness "no man shall see the Lord." Matt. v. 8; Heb. xii. 14. How then is it possible for sinners to go to heaven? He that sins against God wrongs his own soul by unfitting it for heaven, and thus depriving it of celestial blessedness. This a wrong of fearful proportions.

IV. *Sin brings on the soul the miseries of hell.* These miseries include what is meant by "the second death." The first death is that of the body, and is followed by the second death, which begins with the sinner's introduction into eternity. The saint, it is said, "shall not be hurt of the second death." Rev. ii. 11. But how terribly will the lost sinner "be hurt"! What a wrong will he have done to his soul, his own soul—a wrong terrific in its nature, and endless in its duration!

REMARKS.

I. There is great folly as well as wickedness in sin.

II. The sinner is his worst enemy; wrongs his own soul.

III. Hell is a dreadful place; for its inhabitants are moral suicides.

A QUESTION, A COMMAND, AND A PROMISE.

Sirs, What must I do to be saved? And they said, Believe on the Lord Jesus Christ, and thou shalt be saved.—Acts xvi. 30, 31.

It is easy to ask questions, and many trivial questions have been asked in all ages of the world. Men have made inquiries about matters of no moment—matters pertaining to this little world. The question of the text is not trivial; for it concerns salvation. It is the question of a man anxious to be saved. The Philippian jailer was awakened to a sense of his wretched condition, and said: "What must I do to be saved?" We have in the words before us a kind of three-fold theme—

A QUESTION, A COMMAND, AND A PROMISE.

Let us direct our attention to—

I. *The question.* What important things does this question imply?

1. *The sinner's lost condition.* The jailer felt that he was lost. All sinners have transgressed God's holy law. They have brought ruin on themselves. There must be conviction of sin before the question of the text will be asked. Conviction is indispensable. Every one convinced of sin asks: "What must I do?" Conviction has to do with the intellect and the heart. I mean that a man must not only admit in theory, but feel *in his heart*, that he is a sinner.

2. *A sense of the danger to which sin exposes.* Sin is an evil in itself, a great wrong, and on this account ought to be repented of; but there is fearful danger incurred by every sinner. The curse of God's law impends over him, and justice calls for the infliction of the curse. The penalty of the law comprehends all the miseries of hell. The sinner, conscious of his danger, feeling his exposure to the wrath of God, cries out, "What must I do to be saved?"

3. *A deep earnestness about salvation.* The jailer was in earnest. The anxious feelings of his heart prompted his question. If a sinner is ever in earnest, it is when he feels the importance of salvation. What is this world to him then? How little does it appear? He sees his soul unsaved, and an awful eternity before him. He desires above all things to know how he may escape impending wrath and come into a state of acceptance with God.

4. *A willingness to do anything to obtain salvation.* "What must I do?" As if the jailer had said, "I am willing to do whatever is necessary." When a sinner is effectually awak-

ened, he is ready to exert all his powers in securing salvation. He can, it is true, do nothing meritorious, but there is something for him to do, as we shall presently see, and he is willing to do it. His earnestness about salvation makes him willing. So much concerning the question.

II. *The command.* "Believe on the Lord Jesus Christ.' A matter of vital importance is, What is it to believe on Christ? The answer to this question is twofold:

1. *It is to believe what the Scriptures say of his person, and his work of mediation.* If the gospel represents him as the God-man, we do not really believe in him unless we accord to him divinity and humanity. If we say that we can believe in Christ without regard to his person, we make faith a belief in a name rather than in what a name represents. If Jesus died to atone for sin, and we do not consider his death expiatory, we do not in truth believe in him. We divest his death of its most important peculiarity, the very peculiarity which gives it saving power. It is an atoning death.

2. *It is to trust unreservedly in him for salvation.* This is the essence of faith. It is personal trust in a personal Saviour. We sometimes hear faith spoken of as a belief of certain propositions, such as that Jesus Christ is the Son of God, that he died, that he was buried, that he rose from the dead, ascended into heaven. These propositions are vitally important, and they are true; but a simple belief of them does not avail to salvation. There is no saving power in propositions concerning Christ; the power is in Christ himself. There is no power apart from a person. Therefore the faith that saves, is trust in Christ as a personal Saviour. "Believe on the Lord Jesus Christ." The preposition translated *on* seems to suggest the idea of resting the whole weight of our salvation on Christ. Faith is the condition of salvation, not in the sense that it possesses saving merit, but because it brings the believer into union with Christ. The saving virtue

is in him; and when he says to the poor sinner, "Thy faith hath saved thee," the meaning is, that faith is the channel through which saving grace reaches the soul. Notice the words, "to be saved"; not to save myself, but to be saved. After giving himself to Christ in the act of faith, the sinner is *passive*—he is *to be saved.*

III. *The promise.* "Thou shalt be saved." Salvation has to do with the soul and the body, with time and eternity, with earth and heaven. It is accomplished in part in this world, and will be consummated in the world to come. It implies—

1. *Deliverance from sin.* From its condemnation, from its power, from its love, from its pollution, from its practice.

2. *A reparation of all the injuries done by sin.* Sin brought sorrow, suffering, and death into the world. But to the saved, sorrow and suffering are sanctified, and therefore they are blessings in disguise. All the injury that death does by consigning them to the grave will be effectually repaired by the resurrection. To have a glorified body, like that of Christ, will be ample compensation for temporary imprisonment in the grave.

3. *Final exaltation to heaven and immortal blessedness there.* Salvation will reach its culmination and glory at God's right hand.

QUERY.

What do you know about this question, this command, this promise?